A Feast of Flowers

Jacqueline Hériteau

A Feast

of Flowers

Illustrations by Susan Davis

HOUGHTON MIFFLIN COMPANY

BOSTON   NEW YORK

1993

For information about permission to reproduce selections
from this book, write to Permissions, Houghton Mifflin Company,
215 Park Avenue South, New York, New York 10003.

Library of Congress Cataloging-in-Publication Data
Hériteau, Jacqueline.
A feast of flowers / Jacqueline Hériteau ; illustrations
by Susan Davis.
p.   cm.
ISBN 0-395-62884-9
1. Flowers.   2. Flower gardening.   3. Flower arrangement.
4. Seasons.   I.   Title.
SB404.9.H47   1993   93-21792
635.9 — dc20   CIP

Printed in the United States of America

Book design by Kathleen Westray

HOR 10 9 8 7 6 5 4 3 2 1

For my mother, Piney Sutherland Hériteau,
and my husband, Earl Hubbard

Acknowledgments

I AM VERY grateful to my editor Frances Tenenbaum; to publisher Houghton Mifflin; to my agent Gail Ross and her former assistant, Elizabeth Outka, who encouraged me to write these stories and see where they would lead; and to Susan Davis, the artist whose paintings so warmly portray the ideas here.

For their help with various aspects of the book, I am indebted to Susanna Brougham, the manuscript editor; Kathleen Westray, the designer; Charmane Truesdell, president of Dreamscape Associates, Inc., Montpelier, Maryland, whose first love was dried flower arranging; to florist friends Ruth and Peter Darmi, and floral designer Eileen Brennan; to biologist Don Lovness; to paleontologist Peter Kranz; to Holly Shimizu, assistant to the director of the U.S. Botanic Garden; to Dr. Theodore R. Dudley, U.S. National Arboretum; to Dr. A. A. De Hertogh, a devotee of the amaryllis and most knowledgeable about the bulbs that grow well in America; to Sally Ferguson, Netherlands Flowerbulb Institute; to Andre Viette and his wife, Claire, of Viette Nurseries; and to my friend and mentor Dr. H. Marc Cathey, national chair for the Green Industries, USDA.

Contents

Introduction

 ## FLOWERS EVERY DAY

WE GET WHAT WE WANT in life, though it may be a little hard to recognize by the time we get it. Almost always it comes in unexpected ways. When I was eight years old, in the time between lights out and sleep, I used to dream of being Tarzan's Jane, living in a big tree, foraging to feed a brood of babies. There were no apes in my dream, but I saw myself swinging from branch to branch in a jungle which, I realize now, I located by a country road in southern Ontario — rolling farmland rich in mustard and buttercups, Queen Anne's lace, and purple vetch. The big satisfaction, as I recall, was successful foraging in the forest.

Later, having absorbed Mama's stories about life in Paris and at the Château de l'Enardière where I was born — Mama was a Canadian banker's daughter who went abroad and became an opera singer — I changed my dream to writing the Great American Novel in a romantic old country house with an overgrown garden and kids spilling out the windows.

How did life go? Well, not in a direct line, of course.

My youth was divided between my native France and French convents in English-speaking Canada. Later I spent ten years working for a Canadian newspaper, but just as I got my own newspaper column and a radio show, I fell in love with an American editor. I gave up the career, married, and moved to the States. I learned to love a ninety-foot vegetable garden that kept me outdoors till dark;

it produced the fresh vegetables that built my reputation as a cook. Since tending a ninety-foot garden is hard, and I'm greedy for joy, I made space for flowers.

The novels did get written. They're yellowing in the bottom drawer of a file cabinet. But my love for flowers and food has given me thirty published books on gardening and cooking, as well as a good living and a lot of satisfaction.

You can't garden in a tree, but I've gardened almost everywhere else, with coaching from my father, Papa Chéri. *(Cher Papa* is how a dutiful French daughter begins a letter; *Papa Chéri* — Daddy darling — is for coaxing a father you don't know very well because your parents are separated.) I gathered lavender at the château and pulled weeds in Les Sables d'Olonne, my father's village on the Atlantic coast of France. I planted flowers, vegetables, and fruit trees on the roof of a penthouse in Manhattan. I worked huge gardens of vegetables and flowers at a tenant farmer's house in Vermont, a suburban development in Westport, a mansion in northwest Connecticut, and an ancient windswept cottage on Cape Cod. I'm leaving out five or six other gardens, but you can see how it went. As soon as the asparagus patch matured, somehow we had to move.

We ended up here in an old red brick Victorian house in the middle of Washington, D.C. It isn't Tarzan's jungle, but our garden is the closest thing to a flowering woodland glade that you'll find five blocks from the Capitol. Marriage being the way it is these days, two ex-husbands were followed by a permanent one, and between us we have eight children — plus grandchildren — spilling into and out of the in-law apartment downstairs, past the purple plum and peonies, the Easter lilies, the Christmas hollies.

It was flowers that got me through bleak times. At the age of twelve, I would sneak out to the park after Mama fell asleep to steal lilacs and roses for her. I knew exactly what I was doing; I was foraging for one of life's essentials. This was in the late 1930s, the Depression years. We were alone in Canada and broke. Keeping up Mama's *joie de vivre* was as crucial to survival as having air to breathe. Holding flowers, so mysterious in their indomitable unfolding, their fragility and freshness, revived her. Arranging them in a vase saved from happier days in Paris lifted the world for Mama and brought out the sun.

I've come to believe that flowers are a covenant, closer to hand and more tangible than rainbows. Along with family and food, flowers are true substance, the smile of the hidden force that governs all life. Beauty feeds a basic hunger. Joy makes us whole. Everything else is icing on the cake — what you go through to get to the heart of being.

A Feast of Flowers is about having flowers in your life every day.

JACQUELINE HÉRITEAU
Washington, D.C.

PART I

Flowers in Winter

1

Winter's Living Bouquets

FLOWERS IN WINTER seem scarce as raisins in Tante Louise's rice pudding if you don't look in the right places. But there are blossoms to feast on even in an area as wintry as Plainfield, Vermont, when the Winooski River freezes solid, along with the bathroom pipes in old frame farmhouses. Early in the 1960s Harold and I started a new life in one of those, a little tenant farmer's house on the hill across the bridge from town. Our marriage was four years old — our son, Krishna, two. We were just back from a year in Europe, and we were broke. We had stayed in Manhattan only long enough to discover that toddlers playing in Central Park get as sooty as the windowsills; then we headed north, drawn by the promise of clean white snow and a regular salary.

In those days, Plainfield's population was two hundred people and six hundred cows. The main industry was small, avant-garde Goddard College. A grant from the Rockefeller Foundation enabled Goddard to hire Harold, a writer, to help them seek accreditation.

The best month in Plainfield is October. That year the sugar maples flamed yellow, coral, and red, and we drank cider fresh from an apple farm and made apple butter. We baked bread. We feasted with the faculty and students.

November was gray and wet. The green fields and cow pastures surrounding our house faded to gold straw, then to brown furrows. Papa Chéri came from Montreal to help us pull down the stamped tin ceiling, clean up half a century's mouse droppings, and paper and paint the walls. Harold proved allergic to the camel's hair used in the antique plaster walls. A multicolored cat adopted us, had two kittens in an expensive cesarean section, and died.

December was white. In the pumpkin-colored breakfast room, Kris's newly opened Christmas presents made mountains of disorder that spilled into the kitchen. Harold and I disagreed on whether children should be trained to pick up (I was pro) and on most everything else.

January started with three weeks of gray skies and temperatures of minus thirty degrees Fahrenheit. The car door lock froze. The closest plumber was in Montpelier, and when the pipes froze you had to find a friend to lend you a blowtorch to thaw them. Atheneum turned down my novel. Harold gave up on his and started working at the college nights and weekends. The kittens born of the cesarean died. Something like sixty percent of the barn cats in Vermont died that year.

One morning at about seven o'clock the phone rang, and Bijou Richards asked with a joyful whoop, "Is he there yet?" Through the bedroom window I saw the answer dash down the middle of the iron-hard dirt road between snow banks — gray of beard, completely naked in the brightening day. State troopers got him at the bottom of the hill where the road turns left toward the bridge.

Four of us shared a party line, each answering to one, two, three, or four rings. It was like a community conference call and telegraph system. Excitement over the galloping streaker kept us on the line for an hour. Then Farmer Brown's wife went off to bake bread, and another woman hung up to fry eggs for her husband. Bijou felt a bit depressed and said that the poor man always had trouble with the month of January. "We all do," she added, "so bring your kid up this afternoon — I've got two the same."

Bijou lived in a big old farmhouse on the very top of our hill, with a 360-degree view. It was a real farmhouse, though most of the acreage had been sold to Mr. Brown's dairy farm. Her husband, Mark, a big, rangy farmer's son who worked as a librarian at the state capital, had gutted the entire ground floor. A stove and a fridge occupied the far end by the sink; a rectangular wooden table and six folding chairs stood nearby. The kids could do cartwheels in the rest of this plasterboard cavern. There was one beautiful thing: a big green plant spangled with red blossoms in a terra-cotta pot.

Bijou sat the children, whose cheeks and noses were cherry red, in a pool of sun on the floor near the flowers. Sternly she told them they must finish their brown bread and honey sandwiches before they could drink Kool-Aid.

Bijou told me her life story. "I grew up in Brooklyn, and I was going to be a painter; then I came to Goddard College and married Mark." They had both graduated from Goddard.

She also gave me great advice, including the best recipe for canned tuna salad (to a can of tuna, add a minced onion, a handful of minced parsley, a can of peas, chopped celery, hard-boiled eggs, lemon juice, and Hellman's mayonnaise), when in early spring to tap our sugar maples (from mud season until the buds on the maple trees start to swell — late February, March, early April), how much over the posted speed limit was OK with the state police (nine miles per hour), and never to put sugar in someone's gas tank to get even (because the locals wouldn't ever forgive you).

"Why would I do that?" I asked.

"It's what they do here to get even. The sugar ruins everything so you can't drive to work. No transportation, no job, no food. It's murder." I remembered this remark later and decided that either Bijou had known what was going on, or she was prescient.

In the language of flowers, a scarlet geranium means "comforting."

I asked about plumbers, and she said, "Mark's great with plumbing, and you're welcome to call him. Alice Rockland calls him all the time." Alice and her three-year-old son drifted in later. Alice affirmed Mark's plumbing skill. Her husband was a trucker, often away for days. On cold nights, the pipes over at the Rocklands' would freeze up, and Mark always came to her rescue.

Early the sun slid below the window sash, drawing long blue shadows across the white fields. The children's voices ran down. I got Kris into his parka and promised we'd drop in on the Browns to watch the milking. At the door I turned to admire Bijou's flowers. The plant was an ordinary house geranium, the type that stands up and cheers from just about every windowsill in every old stone village in France.

Bijou broke off a gnarly six-inch branch tip, wrapped it in wet newspaper, and handed it to me. "Put it in water in the window," she said. "Roots'll grow, and you can plant it." She laughed at my expression of disbelief. "Just do it — I swear!"

The geranium cutting did what Bijou said it would. I set it in a jelly glass on the sill of one of the kitchen windows. It was a cool, bright place looking northeast past the two bare maples on the lawn and across the dirt road to snow-blanketed meadows and tumbling gray clouds. In a couple of weeks, the cutting put out five thin white roots and slowly enrobed each one in a fuzz finer than silk velvet. Then out shot a skinny stem topped by six scarlet buds, and, one by one, these florets unfolded crimson petals, soft as skin, matte as suede.

Bijou came down the hill to see. "Cut the blossom off," she commanded, "so the strength can go to make roots."

"The flower's the glory," I protested.

"The roots are the power," Bijou said.

We were both right. I have been captive ever since to the magic and mystery, the never-ending bounty and the glory at a gardener's command.

 ## 𝒻LOWERS ℰVERY 𝒟AY

LIVING BOUQUETS

FLOWERS are irrepressible. Roots, seeds, and stem cuttings multiply themselves, like the loaves and the fishes, by enough each year to support the planet. Not only geraniums, but cuttings of wax begonias, browallias, and other garden flowers that we bring indoors when the weather turns to ice will root easily in water and make living bouquets. So will cuttings of the foliage houseplants — pothos, German and Swedish ivy, wandering Jew, spider plant, and many more.

In winter, when everything underground has come to a halt and seems dead, a cutting in a few weeks will spread roots like a living hoop skirt through its vase water. The blossoms put forth by the flowering plants are fewer and smaller than those of plants growing in the garden, but in this gray season they are precious. They promise blue skies, green pastures, and the caress of spring winds.

To thrive, winter cuttings need good light, a cool room, clean vase water, and a drop of fertilizer now and then. Those growing strongly can be potted in soil and moved to the garden when warm weather comes. Under the fringe tree in my kitchen garden, a web of periwinkle is snaking through the pachysandra; it grew from one rooted three-inch cutting. It was part of a little bouquet of *Vinca minor* sprigs and flowers I bought years ago at Eastern Market.

Here are some ways to combine cuttings with greens and odds and ends of florist flowers in small bouquets that thrive on windowsills:

Coleus and Wax Begonias

In fall, bring garden coleus and a few wax begonias indoors to a sunny window — or buy plants from the garden center. When the plants grow leggy, cut off the brightest stems, strip away the lower leaves, arrange them in a large vase, and let them root in water. In late spring, replant the best cuttings outdoors. *Living bouquet:* A bunch of coleus cuttings with two or three bright, bold blossoms from a florist's bouquet.

Browallia

In fall, bring browallias in to a cool spot just out of direct sun — or buy potted browallias. In late winter, root eight-inch tip cuttings in water, and use them as the trailing greens for bouquets. In spring, plant the rooted stems, four to a three-inch pot. *Living bouquet:* Blue browallia with the colored bracts of a fading pink poinsettia.

Geranium

In January, root in water six-inch cuttings of semihardened tips taken from geraniums. They will bloom occasionally through spring. In late spring, plant the rooted stems, three each to five- or six-inch clay pots filled with a gritty soil mix. Move them outdoors as soon as danger of frost is past. *Living bouquet:* Geranium cuttings are pretty with small-leaved ivy, or German or Swedish ivy (all of which will root in water), and a flowering tip of bougainvillea or forced forsythia.

THE CLOROX TRICK

To clean a glass vase that has become clouded, fill it with water and a tablespoon or so of chlorine bleach, and let it soak for about five minutes. The glass will clear.

2

The Belles of Winter

THE GREATEST FLOWER SHOW of the cold months is staged by spring flowering bulbs forced into bloom indoors. Drafty Vermont farmhouses are perfect for forcing; the faculty wives kept alluding to a mysterious fantasia of blossoms in an old farmhouse in the hills. It was lust for a houseful of satiny tulips and daffodils and the sweet, sensual scent of hyacinths that led me to friendship with Bijou's friend Alice.

The vast, elegant old house George Rockland had fixed up for his young wife from the city was across the hill from Bijou and Mark, and full of icy nooks and cool rooms just right for the chilling period that must precede forcing. After the chilled bulbs were planted and rooted, they came into bloom in Alice's main rooms, barely sixty-six degrees Fahrenheit, at a gentle pace. There was time to gloat

over every unfolding inch of leaf and bud. The blossoms lasted ten days, and often more.

I remember Alice's big, almond-shaped, inscrutable black eyes, black hair, and back straight as a poker. Years later, I met Native Americans of the Flathead tribe whose eyes and broad, high cheekbones reminded me of her. She liked to read poetry. Her husband, George, was all Li'l Abner — broad shoulders, brown construction boots, and a big grin. George IV had his dad's sparkling blue eyes and his spirit. He was minus two front teeth, which he lost when he attempted to fly, like Superman, from the tallboy in his parents' bedroom.

On our first visit, Alice gave me a guided tour of abandoned rooms on the second floor, where time-blistered chests and sagging beds were covered with bags and boxes filled with loose bulbs. Some she gave me to feel — round, fat tulips and lumpy daffodils, bulging hyacinths, trim crocuses — while she explained their individual chilling needs. Her best bulbs were kept in the crisper of an old refrigerator, safe from mice and squirrels. She had tried chilling bulbs outdoors, potted and plunged into a covered pit, but when it came time to bring them indoors for forcing, snow and ice had blocked the pits.

When I first toured Alice's bulb works, those she had already potted had completed their chilling period, and with the paperwhites, which didn't need chilling, had been moved downstairs to a huge unused bathroom for the rooting stage. The floor, the raised toilet, footed tub, rusty sink, and overhead shelves were loaded with boxes and pots of dirt, bowls full of pebbles, forcing glasses. Everywhere in the chilly gloom, pointy bulb shoots, like ghostly newborn forests, were growing taller. Alice left for a moment to answer a howl from George IV, and I discovered that this birthing room was also where Alice kept a diary stuffed with letters. It slid to the floor when I reached for a wooden flat of emerging lily-of-the-valley pips. I put the diary back, wondering what it takes to reach the point where you are writing your diary in the bulb room.

When she returned, Alice explained her potting system. The one-pound lard tins filled with pebbles held closely packed daffodils.

Tulips and hyacinths were crowded together in two-pound coffee tins. Thinking of Bijou's husband, Mark, making the long trip over here in the winter night to fix the plumbing, I asked, "Since the pipes freeze, isn't this too cold for rooting?"

"The pipes don't freeze anymore," Alice said crisply, and held out a bowlful of paperwhites rooted in pebbles and water. White-stockinged green stems had stretched up from the bulbs. "The ones in the kitchen have already taken off," she said.

They had. And, like two-stage rockets, they had climbed in a week or two to thirty-six inches and topped themselves with bouquets of ten and more tiny nodding narcissi. Their musky perfume greeted you at every corner, a whiff on the edge of awareness. I measured the stems with Alice's sewing tape. George looked on with a tender, bemused grin.

In mid-February when Kris and I came to call, we found George gone and the master bedroom full of daffodils in bloom — on sills, dressers, night tables, in pools of sun on the bed on George's side — yellow as gold, with that deep, sweet daffodil scent that catches in your throat. The week before, George had come by our house to say goodbye in a way that suggested more than a trucking run. Bijou's car had been in the garage for repairs for a long time. I was driving Bijou to the supermarket, and Mark had to hitch rides to his job.

In late February, the daffodils in Alice's bedroom were replaced by china bowls filled with the charming little cups of yellow and lavender crocuses facing upward. They opened in the noon sun and slowly closed as the winter daylight ebbed. In the kitchen, red and white tulips exposed sooty stamens, and rose and fell with the light on long, sinuous stems. That same month, we helped Alice move dozens of blue and white hyacinths from the bathroom (the diary was gone) into the kitchen. On Good Friday their rich perfume seeped through the house. We sipped wine languidly and stretched out like cats by the fire while a late snowstorm whistled over the hills.

In early March, down-hanging ivory bells opened on frail lily-of-the-valley stems. You must bend to catch their fabulous scent when bloom is forced indoors, but it's there, all right. Alice said it was George's favorite perfume and added that she preferred the smell of the damp earth.

George hadn't come back.

Alice let the bulb foliage ripen on the sills and fertilized the pots until the snow was gone and spring sun had dried the fields by her house. Then she sent the children with me to the edge of the woods to plant the lily-of-the-valley pips, with the hyacinths and some of the hardy small bulbs. She put the remains of the tulips and the paperwhites on the compost pile.

Alice had an impenetrable side, a central separateness always in place as she kneaded bread, sewed buttons, poured red wine in the firelight. Our most animated conversation was late one afternoon in early summer, after the thyme had greened. We walked around the house on the thyme-edged flagstone path to the patio overlooking the valley. Alice described how George had hand-hauled each one of the massive stones from Farmer Brown's north field to make a paved place where she could watch the moon rise while he watched football on television. The scent of the herb was strong. The burning clouds

turned silver, and the cool, bright evening rose around us. Alice pointed out the Big Dipper and the Little Dipper. Her diary was in her lap, her letters to Mark still in it, just where George had found them. Mark never actually saw them. She had said she wanted me to read them so I would know what was in them, but she got lost in the stars and forgot.

Going in to get the kids, Alice told me it was George who had put the sugar in Mark's gas tank before leaving for the islands. George had written to say he was living on a boat and doing plumbing in St. Croix, I believe. In those days, the islands had a great shortage of plumbers, and George had said before he left that he had learned a lot from Mark.

Alice taught us a lot, too — especially this: Never, ever leave letters seeded with longings your husband can't fulfill in a place where he can find them.

THE CONNECTEDNESS OF AN AMARYLLIS

ALL living things are connected by forces the human eye doesn't perceive. People who work with animals sense it. My stepdaughter Alexandra Hubbard Morton once was led safely home through a fog at sea by orca whales. For more than a decade, Alex has been studying the whales near Simoom Sound on the northwest coast of Canada.

Plant people have stories to tell, too. Fran Morris, the wife of the composer John L. Morris, told us a story about a fern that loved her husband. Wherever Fran goes, plants accompany her, but this fern was the only plant John had ever really cared for in Fran's indoor jungle. When their children were young, and John was away in Hollywood doing a movie, he called home every night. On a few occasions when John was on the phone, Fran and their son Evan saw this fern swooningly (her word) wave a frond at the instrument. Fran told me each time she and Evan searched diligently for drafts that could account for the plant's movements. They finally accepted the fact they could find none. Interesting.

My connectedness story is about a potted amaryllis.

Amaryllis is the herald of spring in winter, a huge flowering plant
with character and a nice contrast to the itty-bitty dainties. You
can't walk in quietly with an amaryllis. It's like a trumpet going
down the hall, saying, "Look at me! Look at me! I'm gorgeous!"

People say, "You must be a genius to grow such a thing!"

But with an amaryllis, you know you did practically nothing.
You keep it potbound and lightly fertilized, summer it out in the
sun, and bring it indoors to dry. When it shows signs of growth a
few months later, you remove the dead foliage, water it, and set it
in good light. God does the rest, and multiplies it, too! An amaryllis blooms three to four weeks after it begins to grow, and it
produces offsets regularly. The soaring spathe rises and blooms just
once each year, an appearance anticipated as eagerly at our house as
the first rose, the first asparagus, the first lobster of the season.

Well, one night when I was supposed to be at a church meeting
to shepherd approval for a budget to relandscape the garden, I was

home instead, deep in a conversation with my husband and daughter. The first of the four buds on our amaryllis had just started to break, and I had moved the plant from the window to a black lacquer chest in the middle of the room. As we talked, my attention kept returning to the foliage. One leaf in its fan of twenty-inch, strap-shaped leaves had buckled and was spoiling the symmetry of the amaryllis. Still talking, I got a knife from the kitchen and sawed away at the plant. I turned to find two pairs of eyes, round with amazement, riveted on my hand. I had chopped off the flower scape, not the leaf. The raw edges of the hollow oval stem wept onto the carpet. Me, too.

Shortly after, a church friend telephoned to report that the landscaping money for the garden had been voted down. This budget, which was expected to pass easily, had been cut off out of hand, at just about the time I was chopping off my amaryllis.

The forgiving amaryllis bloomed in a vase by my typewriter. As four giant crimson buds opened one after the other, I discovered what we all now know: the amaryllis is a great cutting flower. The new pink and melon varieties and the red-edged whites turn up regularly in those huge floral arrangements in the wall niches at the Metropolitan Museum of Art in New York and in lobby arrangements in luxury hotels. The cut flowers are stunning combined with giant tulips, branches of forced pink apple blossoms, white dogwood, purple magnolias with cream interiors, magnolia cones, and big, brown-backed magnolia leaves.

FLOWERS EVERY DAY

AMARYLLIS FANTASIES

THE scale and drama of a potted amaryllis invite you to create a special setting for the plant. Don't hide it until it blooms, or after. Long before the flower opens, you have the nurturing green. A soaring fan of leaves develops as the flowering stem rises and remains after the bloom is over — rich, textural, awe-inspiring. I love to see an amaryllis growing in an ancient tin box or a scarred pewter pot. This green magnificence rising from a time-battered container reminds you that though we seem to fall apart, beauty is a constant. Here are some ways to show off your amaryllis:

· Line an old wicker basket with plastic or foil and set into it a pot containing a dusky orange-red or deep red amaryllis. Fill in with potting mix. Press tall Scotch broom into the soil on one side to create a frame for the plant. On the other side, stand some bear grass flowing toward the broom. Cover the soil with damp green sheet moss.

· Arrange two pots of amaryllis in a window box, and fill the spaces between with house-plants. Some should cascade — for instance, ivy (English, Swedish, or German), pothos, spider plant, philodendron, wandering Jew, striped inch plant. Some should be upright — for instance, young dracaena, screw pine, baby snake plant, sweet flag, aloe, or variegated St. Augustine grass. With the amaryllis soaring above all, you have the high, middle, and low elements of ikebana — sky, humanity, earth — the three levels that combine to bring delight.

· Line a deep basket with plastic or foil, set into it three pots of developing amaryllis, and fill partially with potting mix. At each end, plant small-leaved ivy trained to cascade over the edges. Press tall, skinny water glasses into the soil between the pots of amaryllis, and pack potting mix around them. When the amaryllis blooms go by, fill the glasses with seasonal flowers. Or, fill the spaces between the amaryllis with Christmas greens. When the greens deteriorate, pack the area with dozens of sprouted paperwhites. Follow with primroses.

· On a big table, arrange seven amaryllis — one already beginning to bloom in the center, flanked by others not yet ready. Arrange pots of ferns and variegated small-leaved ivy at varying heights among the amaryllis.

· Set five potted amaryllis on the floor in front of a bright window, and surround them with potted ferns. They will reach for the light, and soon the bottom of the window will fill with greens. They will take your breath away as stems and leaves come zooming up, followed by big beautiful flowers that reach up as if to drink the sky.

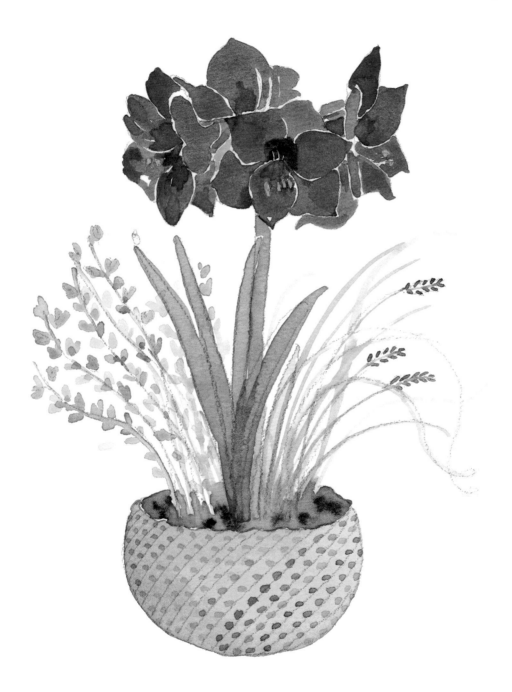

3

Branches That Bloom Indoors

GREAT BUNDLES of flowering branches, dewy as spring, fragrant as rain, are glorious when the snow is deep and white out there, and nature looks as though it will never wake up. They are ours for forcing: cut as the buds begin to swell in late winter or early spring, provided with humidity and warmth, seemingly lifeless buds will open and unfold small blossoms and dainty green leaves — as though a very shy spring had arrived. As magical as the rooting of a cutting and the winter blooming of spring bulbs, this process is also called "forcing."

Most flowering shrubs and trees respond to forcing. Among the finest are the flowering cherry, deep coral quince, pink crabapple,

SWEDISH ECSTASY

and white dogwood. Forsythia, my favorite, is ready to force very early, and the color is pure spring sunshine. Its leaves — scraps of green — poke out as the blossoms fade so the bouquet remains attractive for weeks. I've had forsythia branches root and, planted, live on in the garden. Pussy willows, cut before the buds swell, provide weeks of delight. Even without flowers, fresh new leaves are a promise of spring; well-budded stems from saplings and shrubs will leaf out airily.

The branches that flower most fully are those at the top of the plant. They produce the most flower buds and have the closest flower-bud spacing. Florists sometimes remove leaf buds to focus more attention on the blossoms. Flower buds are easy to recognize: they're larger. Cut the stems at a sharp angle. If you're taking branches from a friend's garden or the woods, and won't be putting them into water for hours or a day or two, bundle them in plastic to keep them from drying out. Store the bundles in a cool place. Recut the stem ends before you begin forcing.

There are at least two schools of thought about what to do next. There's a simple cold method for forcing, and there's a warm method. Whichever you choose, wash the forcing containers well, and put a little chlorine bleach in the final rinse.

I learned the cold method for forcing branches in Sweden, where winters and winter nights are even longer than they are in Canada. The year before we moved to Vermont, we spent many weeks in Sweden in the rolling blue hills of Dalecarlia. There we bought troll dolls, saw a snowstorm in June, made mayonnaise for a countess, and danced around a Maypole decked with blossoms. We also experienced midsummer's night in Old Town Stockholm. On June 21, the night of the summer solstice when the sun hardly sets before it rises, the whole city goes into ecstasy. Shops decorate their entrances with young trees sprouting new, pale leaves. I was amazed that any remained in the country after the celebration.

On one of our late-winter visits, we spent several days in a country home that had the quality of encapsulated spring. We were more aware of the flowering or leafed-out branches than of the furniture.

SECRET LIVES

Buds begin to develop in summer, and by the middle of fall, they are completely formed though still rather insignificant. As day length grows in January and February, the buds begin to swell, and that's when we first notice them. But completely formed new life has been there all along, waiting for spring warmth to open it for its day in the sun.

Everything was pale green or pale gold. I recall one room that held just a loom, a magnificent thing in golden wood strung with wool the white of clean sheep, and a few ceiling-high branches of apple blossoms. The fat buds were breaking and scraps of creamy pink were spilling out.

I also remember a long hall, its south side set with floor-to-ceiling windows looking over a lawn. The lawn was studded with young trees from the encroaching forest, and it sloped to a lake that reflected puffy white clouds. The trees were still bare. Forsythia, planted to hide the foundation of the house, scratched at the windows.

Lunch was steamed salmon served with fresh mayonnaise and mounds of small, crisp, salted potatoes garnished with chopped fresh dill. I had peeled the potatoes. It is a law in Sweden that potatoes appear at every meal and that one of the lady guests peels them, for the hands of all hostesses without exception are allergic to potato peelings.

After lunch, in heavy sweaters and rubber boots, we walked to a patch of snow on the north side of the woods and filled old pails with the wet, grainy stuff. Then the men attacked the forsythia thicket under the hall windows. They removed about a quarter of the oldest limbs from each shrub, leaving the arching main branches clear. As they worked, our hostess explained how a portion of the hedge was harvested for forcing every week or so, from late winter until the job was done.

Not all the prunings were shapely enough to bring indoors. The best budded branches were trimmed back to two to three feet in length. Stuck into the snow in our pails, they rested two days in a cool, dark storeroom off the garage. Then we filled tall vases with cool water, recut and arranged the branches in the vases, and set them in the sun along the window-lined hall. At noon, the glass seemed to disappear and the forsythia appeared to float on air.

When I remarked that the shorn hedge had paid a price for our pleasure, I was shushed. Years later in Connecticut, I discovered that pruning during the dormant season results in a vigorous burst

In the language of flowers quince means "temptation."

FLORAL NAMETAGS

In Sweden, our friends often worked out seating arrangements at dinner by inviting each guest to choose one flower from a bouquet and match it to a blossom floating in a small crystal dish at the table. The men chose from one bouquet and the women from the other, then they matched up the flowers.

of growth in spring. Left unpruned, forsythias grow into impenetrable thickets with few blossoms — great for hiding small children, or rabbits escaping from dogs and cats.

The warm method is the one used by my friend Marc Cathey, a former director of the U.S. National Arboretum. For forcing, Marc places branches in water at bath temperature — 90 to 110 degrees Fahrenheit. Marc wraps the branches and the whole container in sheets of plastic and sets them in a dim, warm room overnight. This high-humidity, high-temperature environment gets the sap flowing. Warmth and humidity also encourage the dry scales covering the flower buds to expand and activate dormant buds.

There's a third way to force branches — just put them in water in a sunny place without any particular preparation, and they'll bloom.

Whichever forcing method you choose, monitor the water levels in the containers. The branches transpire greatly as they develop, and the water requires topping at least twice a week. There's no need to use florist's flower-keeping chemicals for forcing as long as the vases and water are very clean.

 *Flowers Every Day*

YOU can have flowering branches blooming indoors from late winter through midspring. The time to cut the branches for forcing is when the buds, those tight little nubbins encased in scales, begin to swell. The dates on the table below suggest when to look at your shrubs to see if the buds are swelling.

Each shrub or tree has its own individual wake-up call, programmed to respond to the amount of daylight it is receiving, how warm it is, and how long it has been warm. Here on Capitol Hill in Washington, D.C., forsythia is ready to cut for forcing in late January or mid-February; it varies from year to year. Just down the road, on certain protected south-facing slopes of the National Arboretum — and in regions farther south — forsythia buds swell two or three weeks earlier. I remember that the buds swell near New York City more often in late February, two to three weeks earlier than in Westport, Connecticut, an hour or so northeast.

TIMETABLE FOR
FORCING BRANCHES

The time the branches will require to go from bud stage to blooming varies according to when you cut. Cut very early, forsythia can take three weeks to open its sunny little flags. Cut later, when the buds are very full, they could open in just a week.

Plants	When to Cut for Forcing	Forcing Time	Bloom Period
Forsythia	Early January to mid-March	1–3 weeks	7 days
Flowering plum	Late January	3–4 weeks	10 days
Flowering peach	Late January	4–5 weeks	7 days
Flowering cherry	Late January to mid-March	2–4 weeks	7–14 days
Flowering pear	Late January to mid-March	2–5 weeks	7–14 days
Japanese quince, flowering quince	February to mid-March	2–5 weeks	4–7 days
Willow*	February	1–2 weeks	Indefinite, if allowed to dry
Lilac	Early March	4–6 weeks	3–7 days
Dogwood	Mid-March	2–4 weeks	7–10 days
Apple, crabapple	Mid-March	2–3 weeks	7 days
Bridal wreath	Mid-March	2–3 weeks	7–10 days

* Remove the scales from the buds. When the furry tips are full, empty the vase, or the stems will root and drop buds.

4

Snow Blossoms and Sun Scents

FROM MANSION TO TRAILER in Plainfield, Vermont, everyone had an indoor winter garden. The clouds were high, the air clear as crystal on the coldest days. The sun in winter made a low arch across the sky; its light bounced off the snow and shone right into our windows, turning the sills into little greenhouses. With hot air blasting by day, nights cooled to save fuel, and untamed drafts to provide moist, fresh air, ours were environments in which tropical and semitropical flowers produced extravagantly.

I still remember the first flowering houseplants I acquired. There was an African violet that put up slender sprigs covered with rich purple blossoms; a cyclamen with flowers like swept-back wings; a gardenia as lavishly fragrant as a whole bottle of perfume; and,

THE GREAT VIRTUE
OF SWEET SMELLS

ELEGANT CYCLAMEN

Cyclamen has elegant, taffetalike, scalloped leaves topped by long-lasting blooms on sinuous stems, like Tinker Bell in a steep dive, wings swept back. A mature plant in full bloom anchors a buffet table beautifully. Set a pink cyclamen plant in a pale green cachepot, and surround it with shiny red cherries or rosy strawberries with their stems on. (To keep the strawberry stems fresh, mist them before placing the berries on the table.) For a small table, arrange a few cyclamen flowers and a leaf or two in an ikebana holder or a small vase, and cluster small rosy fruits around the base.

of course, the geraniums and wax begonias Bijou taught me to multiply. Later, I came to know an easy orchid, *Oncidium*, which bears tiny dancing-doll blooms on an arching stem, and sun-loving, sweet blue heliotrope, which, to my surprise, is only one of the many flowers that prefer to be potbound. Eventually, I collected the beautiful foliage plants, some as colorful as flowers — poinsettias, sun-loving crotons, coleus, variegated pothos and ivy, ferns. In Plainfield we used everything — clippings, blossoms, potted plants — to make living centerpieces for our kitchen *soirées*.

One of Vermont's few environmental sins was that it shut us away for too many months from the good smells of the earth and rain, the trees and fields. Eventually one wearies of *eau de radiator* and essence of dust balls. But by our second year, faculty wives had taught me that watering lots of houseplants produces heady whiffs of that good after-rain smell. I learned on my own the sensual pleasure of sharing my shower with a big hibiscus — the shower refreshes the hibiscus, scales down its white fly population, and above all, releases scent of forest floor.

When we lived in Vermont, maturing an indoor forest was a hobby. Now NASA research has shown that the most efficient way to provide fresh air for space stations is to use plants for purification and renewal. You'd think someone would have noticed earlier that that's how the planet does it — but never mind. Flowering plants that are some of the best air scrubbers include mums, florist's azaleas, and orchids; highly rated foliage plants are the bromeliads, *Draceana marginata*, pothos, poinsettias, *Ficus benjamina*, and spider plant.

Fine as the foliage plants are, in Plainfield we had an eye for beauty and a nose for scent. Our floor gardens included fragrant flowers and herbs, such as the scent-leaved geraniums. Strategically placed near the phone or the cookie jar, where you brush or pat them as you pass, herbs arrest mind static. Their scents remind you that every day life is new. As for the flowering plants — ah, the flowers. When it's been white out there for four months, nothing compares with the thrill of seeing buds begin to swell. A bud breaks, showing a pale line, and leaves you waiting breathless for the grand opening. Then you awaken one morning to a whisper of gardenia in the air.

Many naturally fragrant blossoms are quite modest in appearance, compared to the showy gardenia — for example, heliotrope, stock, mignonette, wallflowers, tuberose. The strongest fragrances are usually found in flowers that are white, palest yellow, or pink. But there are lots of exceptions, such as purple-blue hyacinths and purple petunias.

AFTER you've grown indoor plants on the windowsill for a while, and especially if you summer them outdoors (in shade or partial sun, please, or they'll sunburn), they grow up to be shrubs and trees. Grouped indoors in front of a sunny window, they become a floor garden — easier to maintain and fun to look at.

The first thing a floor garden needs is a waterproof floor. I drag from house to house the 3-by-3½-foot zinc tray I had made at a hardware store. (Right now it's acting as the roof for my potting table in the back yard.) A large boot tray will do. Line the tray with an inch or two of coarse, clean gravel. Keep water in the bottom of the tray at all times, but make sure the water level is not so high that the pots are actually standing in water.

Here are two floor gardens using popular houseplants:

FRAGRANT FLOOR GARDENS

For a Big, Sunny Window

· Next to the window, set a hibiscus and fragrant flowering plants such as gardenia, sweet olive, and jasmine.

· Add a bold foliage plant such as *Dieffenbachia,* Chinese evergreen, umbrella plant, or coleus. (The umbrella plant does need to sit in a dish of water.)

· In spots with less light, arrange ferns.

· Stand a ficus tree or a tall rubber plant to one side of the window, and use a corn plant (*Dracaena* 'Massangeana') to join the trees to the tray plants.

In the language of flowers,
heliotrope means
"devotion."

· In early winter, keep forced paperwhites and hyacinths up front, away from direct sun.

· Follow these with vases of flowering branches, and later with pansies or scented primroses.

· When seedlings for annuals become available, enjoy them here for a few days before moving them outdoors.

For a Cool Room and Filtered Light

· Set out low-growing plants such as bird's-nest fern, 'Fluffy Ruffles' Boston fern, rabbit's-foot fern, and ivy.

· Vary the heights by setting some of the ferns on upended pots.

· Among the ferns, tuck in pots of fragrant seasonal flowers, forced paperwhites, blue and white hyacinths, or scented primroses.

· In spring, bring in fragrant seedlings headed for the garden — wallflowers, purple petunias, pinks, heliotrope, sweet alyssum, nicotiana, mint, basil, oregano, thyme, eucalyptus.

MAMA LOVED GARDENIAS

MAMA smelled of freshly washed wool sweaters and Players cigarettes, and she especially loved the perfume and the white velvet opulence of gardenias. When we moved to Ottawa, we lived in a two-bedroom walkup near the streetcar barns on the wrong side of Sandy Hill. Mama furnished the place with the massive, ornate Louis XIV pieces saved from the château and with gold and purple velvet drapes. The wallpaper pattern repeated long-tailed, golden birds of paradise perched in gold trees against a gold and purple jungle. There was an upright piano and an ancient typewriter, and the walls were lined with shelves of leather-bound French poetry (Mama's library), and Bibles and nineteenth-century philosophers (Grandmother Sadie Agnes's books). The British schoolgirl magazines featuring illicit midnight feasting on cucumber sandwiches and pickles were mine. Mama made superb apple pie, gave voice lessons to the sons and daughters of old friends, and wrote novels to revive our fortunes (they didn't). Now and then a famous friend

from Mama's Paris days turned up with a gardenia corsage and took
her to dinner at the Château Laurier. The year I was ten, it was José
Iturbi, the pianist.

When Mama came home, we unwound the green florist's wrap-
pings from her gardenia, and she trimmed an inch off the stem and
put the blossom in a cut-glass bonbon dish. Covered by a bowl, the
flower was stored in the refrigerator and stayed fresh and headily
fragrant for days. We took it out at dinner each day. Mama lit
candles and told stories about the great days in Paris and Biarritz
when she was married to Yves Nat, the pianist. He was her husband
before Papa Chéri. In those years, she had been dressed by Worth
and her Russian chef created fabulous floral centerpieces for her
parties. She said he was a melancholy man who played the violin
and drank too much. After he left, Mama discovered that the
centerpieces stood upright because they were tied to forms he had
nailed into her dinner table. Mama's stories drowned the screeching
of streetcars rounding our corner, and the room was full of fragrant
blossoms, wise playwrights, beautiful actresses and demimondaines,
interesting crooks, noble peasants, and philosophic chauffeurs.

I float the first gardenia of the season in a crystal bowl on my breakfast tray. Blooms that come later I leave among the leaves to wilt to gold; I'm always awed that I have midwifed such sumptuous events. The extraordinary gardenia scent — the only floral that can't be extracted for perfume, I've heard — lingers until the very end.

Flowers are like Mama — their beauty is vulnerable and they know it, yet they unfold it with unshakable trust in the very eye of the storm.

FLOWERS EVERY DAY

LIVING CENTERPIECES

HALF the fun of a dinner party is foraging for flowers that will make the table festive. I love centerpieces that include treats. Nibbling on the decor anchors family and friends to the table, and real conversations happen.

Edibles for a Centerpiece

· Clusters of green seedless grapes are perfect with anything floral, and purple grapes are indescribably luscious with crimson and pink flowers.

· Cherries, strawberries with the stems on, large, perfect raspberries, golden-orange kumquats, and Lady apples enhance flowers in the red, pink, and orange range.

· Chocolates wrapped in silver or gold foil add sparkle to everything.

· Brown nuts in their shells add an earthy note. Be sure to include nutcrackers.

· Dried dates, figs, prunes, and apricots have a homespun beauty; stuffed with peanut butter and dusted with confectioners' sugar, dates become a gala confection.

Houseplants

· Flowering houseplants make fine centerpieces when set in cachepots or dressed in sparkling white tissue paper with satin bows the color of the flowers. African violets, sunny kalanchoes, brilliant bougainvilleas, blue Persian violets all look good. On a large buffet table use cyclamen in full bloom. The foliage of the new hybrids is like watered silk, and the flowers bloom in profusion.

· Use small green houseplants to center the table — small-leaved green or variegated English ivies, pothos, peppers, coleus, baby ferns. Press into the soil flower vials garnished with flowers from houseplants or a florist's bouquet — a cyclamen, a daffodil, the side bud of a mum, a streptocarpus flower.

Background Greens

· Use sprigs of arborvitae, hemlock, or spruce; clusters of needles from white pine; leaves of aucuba, nandina, magnolias, or camellias.

· Evergreen cones, large and small, are hand-

some in their natural colors or splashed with white or silver florist's spray paint.

· In mild regions, the hardy garden herbs — variegated thyme, sage, lemon verbena — yield up a sprig or two of fragrant greens.

Seedlings in Bloom

· Primroses and pansies

· Large-flowered wax begonias, English daisies

· Impatiens, petunias, marigolds

with

· Clustered pots of baby mints, thymes, chives, oreganos, purple and green basils, lavenders, lemon verbena.

· Dusty miller, lamb's-ears *(Stychys byzantina)*, young caladiums, small coleus, epimediums, sedums. (All are attractive coupled with white flowers.)

These garden-fresh centerpieces are especially attractive in simple kitchen and garden containers. Include clippings and prunings from porch planters, friends' gardens, the fields, the market.

Slat Box of Primroses

A wooden flat made of slats can hold six primrose or pansy seedlings in bloom: lavender, pink, purple, yellow, white, rosy-red. Fill with green sprigs — ficus tips, pachysandra, hemlock.

Terra-cotta Miniature Planter with Pansies

In a small rectangular terra-cotta planter, set three pansy seedlings in shades of imperial pink, or primroses. Fill with tufts of something silvery, like dusty miller, white pine, verbascum.

Bread Basket with Herbs

In a long, narrow bread basket, place six pots of herb seedlings. Fill with flowered sprigs of forsythia, quince, cherry, or apple blossoms.

Round Basket of Impatiens

In a large, round, shallow basket, arrange six or eight seedlings of red and white dwarf impatiens. Fill with green trailing stems of vinca, oregano, and mint.

Bowl of Petunias

In a white bowl, arrange seedlings of red, white, and blue petunias. Fill with sprigs of small-leaved ivy, trailing vinca, or lemon verbena.

SCENTED GERANIUMS

Scented geraniums bring the aroma of fresh herbs indoors, and they grow well in a pot on a sunny sill indoors as well as in a hanging basket or a window box outdoors. Their blossoms are modest compared to the big zonal geraniums, but the fragrant oils in the foliage confer a lasting scent of nutmeg, mint, rose, or lemon. The strongest aroma is in the plants that have small white or pale pink blossoms. Dried leaves are used in potpourris — my grandmother would place a single fresh leaf in the bottom of the glass to flavor certain delicate jellies. In New Zealand, native land of the scent-leaved geranium, a fresh leaf is placed under a cake or a pudding before baking. Sugar is layered with the leaves, and bundles of the leaves are used to polish wooden bowls and utensils. Each of the popular species has a distinct aroma, and they are a delight grown together as a collection. They draw you again and again to squeeze and compare!

Lemon Geranium

Pelargonium crispum, nice in finger bowls, has small, crinkly leaves with a lemony scent. The flowers are two-toned pink. Varieties recommended by experts are 'Prince Rupert', 'Mable Grey', and 'Lemon Fancy'.

Rose Geranium

Pelargonium graveolens is grown commercially for its sweet-scented essential oils. The most popular of the scented geraniums, its rose-lavender flowers are blotched dark purple in the middle of the upper petal.

Apple Geranium

Pelargonium odoratissimum has small, velvety, sweetly scented, ruffled leaves and bears white flowers. 'Gray Lady Plymouth' is a pretty, variegated plant.

Peppermint Geranium, Woolly Geranium

Pelargonium tomentosum has large, soft, fuzzy, grapelike leaves and tiny purple-veined white flowers.

PART II

$\mathcal{F}$LOWERS
in $\mathcal{S}$PRING

5

Hills of Daffodils and Lilacs

FLOWERS IN SPRING are as plentiful as calories in an ice cream sundae. In April in Washington, D.C., you can sit lazy on the curb and not do a darn thing — petals from the cherry blossoms and roses will fall all over themselves to get to you. The first dainty bulb flowers take over our Capitol Hill garden in February, just after the witch hazels bloom down the road at the National Arboretum. Next thing, hyacinths and daffodils are yellowing under the azaleas, catbirds have finished their love songs, and the gray squirrels are scolding their young behind a wall of dark green leaves.

Bloom times get muddled here in Washington's illogical climate. To learn the true sequences of spring flowering, go to the hills. Where spring is long and slow and wet, where nights are crisp, the

In the language of flowers,
a red tulip means
"declaration of love."

spring flowers — which are cool-season bloomers — can linger through their full flowering season safe from the blasting effect of unseasonable heat. For two wonderful years we rented a place like that, an unmanicured estate called Okeden where just about every flower you ever wanted had been planted and left to naturalize.

Kris was eight, and Holly and David — ages two and nine months, respectively — were still called the "Weensies" when we moved to Sharon, a beautiful little town in the foothills of the Berkshires, west of the Housatonic River. Most of its farms had been transformed by waves of artists, writers, and moneyed New Yorkers.

Okeden, and the small meadows above and below it, is next to the Buckley compound on Main Street. The original house was built in the 1700s of pink-coral brick, and the wooden extension and the barn were painted a deep rosy pink. The white iron gingerbread framing the porch came much later, but it was put in place before the wisteria had reached the top floor and before the climbing hydrangea had been planted by the front entrance. Ancient maples, evergreens, and the biggest tulip tree in Connecticut shaded the grounds. When the tulip tree bloomed, we rushed up to the attic for a better view of the huge, sky-high, greenish yellow blossoms. The attic — a wonderful, echoing place — sheltered the top of the wisteria vine, which had worked its way through a crack in the window frame.

In the beginning, I hated the taste of the late, great decorator who had owned the place. The rooms were *all* pink and green.

"You'll grow into it," my husband said.

"Hah!" I said, busy with the outdoors, which had a lot of pink and green, too.

In late March and April, blossoms filled the air. Hedges covered themselves with golden forsythia, and dainty white flowering plum and pink cherry trees came into bloom. Spiraea spilled its bridal whites and was followed by the sprawling coral-pink Japanese quinces. In late April, a pretty little hawthorn in the meadow below the house bloomed cerise-pink, while the apple trees between Route 4 and the front door covered themselves with fragrant pink-white flowers that buzzed with honeybees. Late afternoons were perfumed by the lavender lilac hedge. Then the ancient honeysuckles behind Okeden made the air sweet. In early summer, hummingbirds came to hover over the trumpet vine on the trellis by the dining room door.

As the shrubs unfolded their flowers, spring-blooming bulbs carpeted the earth. The frost was hardly out of the ground when fragrant white and purple hyacinths came up by the dining room door, and in the tall grass beyond the honeysuckles, the small, early-blooming bulbs made runs and trills. In drifts of twenty, fifty, and a hundred, we came to know winter aconite, snowdrops, species crocuses, miniature daffodils. Glory-of-the-snow and the first blue-bells bloomed. Where nothing else was happening, early, midseason, and late, wild daffodils splashed the greens with gold. A ribbon of lily-of-the-valley unfurled green flags, and on the first of May our children made perfumed nosegays to give away.

Fronting what had been the vegetable garden behind the barn, a straggly row of tulips came up, and five kinds of mint hid the stone

A PENNY
FOR YOUR TULIPS

Pennies in the vase water for tulips seems to prolong their life. Some people say "nonsense" — but it works for me.

steps. Old-fashioned bleeding-heart hung valentines by a path edged with bellflowers, bright pink cranesbill, and 'Crater Lake Blue' veronica. In the shade of the trees screening us from Route 4, a carpet of grass finer and softer than any I'd ever seen came up, later edged baby-blue by forget-me-nots.

There was much more! The dining room windows looked out over a formal garden centered by a weathered birdbath. Four L-shaped beds surrounded it, each corner anchored by sprawling gray spears of huge yucca, which I first hated and later loved for the very boldness I had hated. The rest of the plantings had gone gloriously wild with help from the birds, the bees, the squirrels, the wind. As the first bulbs faded, candytuft banked the sides of the beds with white, and in shaded places, wild purple and white columbine nodded above foliage as dainty as maidenhair fern. In May, the driveway was lined with hedges of white peonies. We filled the rooms with huge, pungent bouquets of peonies in pink, rose, purple-red, white-flecked red. In mid-June, the Siberian irises bloomed for several coolish weeks, then disappeared, leaving spear-like foliage as a backdrop to tangles of sooty-hearted, silken Oriental poppies. Creeping baby's-breath spent the early summer reclaiming its territory under the lavender bushes in the rose beds.

There was more, all wonderfully Old World, like a classical painting cracked and crazed with the Garden of Eden growing up through it. Whenever I encountered the spirit of the former owner, I apologized for my rash first impressions of her taste. I would say, "I had no idea!"

An impulse drove me to dust the tops of the china cabinets in the pantry, not one of my ingrained habits, and there I discovered frogs and vases in every size and shape, and woven containers that inspired us to make floral baskets for Easter. I came across faded notes in old cookbooks, at the bottom of drawers in the servants' rooms, in the former owner's library collection of Napoleona. They were written in a spidery, elegant hand:

"Evening stock is the one for fragrance — but very difficult to grow from seed. Buy seedlings."

"Fuchsias love the cool nights here at Okeden!"

"Phosphorus! Oh, how desperately our American soils need phosphates!"

"I would have liked to be Josephine at Malmaison."

LILY-OF-THE-VALLEY is an enduring woodland native of both Eurasia and North America. The leaves start out looking like tiny green umbrellas, then they unfurl, and up comes a dainty stem hung with exquisite downward-facing bells. The perfume is pure joy. Forced into bloom indoors, the lily-of-the-valley flower is modest to insignificant, but I do it for love and memories.

In summer when I was a child, we drove from Château de l'Enardière to Le Havre and crossed the Atlantic on one of those great old ocean liners to visit my widowed grandmother, Sadie Agnes Sutherland. She lived in Winchester, Ontario. Tall, elegantly curved, and blond, Sadie Agnes smelled of lavender and lemon. She always wore something lavender — a handkerchief, a scarf, a bunch of flowers on the brim of a big hat. The house Daniel Fraser Sutherland had built for her when Canada was new was called The Maples, a white Victorian with a bay window, red trim, and gingerbread. The year I turned three I learned to speak English, and Grandmother Sadie Agnes let Mama and me plant lily-of-the-valley under the mock orange and the purple lilac in the flower border.

In the time it took me to get from age three to age seven, Sadie Agnes had turned the Sutherland bank over to a manager, married the British diplomat she fell in love with, and moved to London. We went broke in the Depression, the bank manager committed suicide, my parents separated, the château and The Maples were sold, Mama and I moved to Ottawa, and I got shipped off to a convent as a boarder. But the lily-of-the-valley prospered. It carpeted the humus-rich ground around the lilac and ducked under the white trellis fence into the churchyard. As Mama and I said goodbye forever to childhood and security, the lily-of-the-valley was marching triumphantly down Main Street, yard to yard to yard, aided and abetted by our former neighbors.

RITE OF SPRING

In the language of flowers, lily-of-the-valley stands for the return
of happiness. In France, it blooms in late April and early May, in
time for *la fête du muguet,* an ancient ritual celebrating the reappear-
ance of flowers. On May 1, millions of nosegays of lily-of-the-valley
and their leaves are sold by flower vendors and given to lovers,
friends, and coworkers.

I can date precisely my first encounter with *la fête du muguet.*
When World War II ended, Mama sent me back to France to
complete my education. On the night of May 1, 1949, near the
Deux Magots in the Latin Quarter, Akos Biro, an artist refugee
from Communist Hungary, snatched the nosegay I was reaching for
from the vendor's tray, the last one she had. Disappointed, I went
on into the bistro to meet the friends I had wanted to give the
flowers to. Akos came in behind me, set the bouquet before me on
the table, and kissed my hand with all the panache of his passionate
Magyar ancestors.

 # FLOWERS EVERY DAY

EASTER BASKETS AND BOUQUETS

Easter Baskets

At Okeden we learned to make a spring garden in a basket. Potted flowering bulbs, houseplants, young annuals, and foliage plants grow well together by the doorstep or on a bright windowsill in a well-aired room.

Shortly before Easter, garden centers are loaded with pots of bulbs breaking into bloom and flowering seedlings. Primroses and pansies are followed by flats of petunias, salvias, impatiens. For foliage contrast, include young green plants — ferns, small-leaved ivy, small houseplants, and their cuttings. Young herbs and scented geraniums add a rich fragrance.

The basket can be any shape or size — round, square, oval — as long as it is at least six inches deep; eight or ten inches is better if tall bulbs are among the plantings. If it has a hinged lid, leave it open; if the lid is detached, prop it beside the basket. Line the basket with a sheet of heavy-duty plastic or foil large enough to reach the rim. Spread a two-inch layer of small pebbles over the bottom, then fill halfway to the top with damp potting mixture.

Remove the plants, including the bulbs, from their pots and crowd the plants in the basket — that makes a prettier display and helps the bulb flowers stay upright. Settle the largest flowers first. Tuck edgers and cascading greens into the basket front and along its outer edges. Plant the middle ground last, then fill the basket with potting mix. Press the plants gently into place. Water lightly now and for the life of the basket.

The bulb flowers will be the first to fade. Remove the flower stems but keep the foliage until it becomes unattractive, then cut it off. When all the bulbs have gone by, plant flowering seedlings of summer annuals right on top of them.

Here are Easter basket combinations that suggest the range of materials you can fit into baskets of various sizes and shapes:

A BLUE, SQUARE, EIGHT-INCH BASKET

(Match the basket color.)
For height: four seedlings of blue pansies, purple primroses, or something similar.
Filler: pairs of herb seedlings — curly parsley and tarragon, for instance, or lemon verbena and thyme.
Edgers: six young plants of low-growing Greek oregano, or silver variegated thyme.

A DEEP, SQUARE, TEN-INCH BASKET

For height: two small Boston ferns, or other greens.

Filler: six miniature irises or daffodils for the center.

Edgers: eight small bulbs and two small-leaved ivies, or variegated vinca, for the front.

A LOW, ROUND, SIX-INCH-DIAMETER BASKET

For height: twelve grape hyacinths, or two young Persian violets.

Filler: six johnny-jump-ups or small pansies.

Edgers: six low, dainty foliage plants such as baby's-tears or creeping fig.

Bouquets, Ribbons, and Bows

The gardens at Okeden formed my taste in bouquets, just as Mama, Papa Chéri, and family
members who cherish fine food formed my palate.
I love any flower and just about any floral combi-
nation, but I see most elegance in bouquets created by the wheel of the seasons. I like them
embellished by seasonal companions and — well,
yes, a little silk and satin to enhance the color and
shine.

About trimmings: the better the quality of the
ribbon, the nicer the effect. Ribbons in real silk
and double-sided satin are the finest. Yard goods
shops hold remnant sales after the holidays, and I
stock up on the most useful colors in quarter-inch
widths. A few yards of each desirable shade in
widths ranging up to 2½ inches are sure to get
used up, too. And when I see leftovers in ribbons
3½ to 4 inches wide in rare shades of mauve,
ivory, or sage green, I buy them. I look also for
fabric remnants to cut into ribbons. The color of
a flower repeated in a superb print adds a certain
cachet.

Craft shops and florist supply centers offer glit-
tery things — silver and gold ribbons, plaid, tar-
tan, and special effect ribbons such as French
ribbon, which is wired on its outer edges for
shaping into bows. Curling ribbon, a quarter-
inch wide or more, is festive all by itself. The
quarter-inch width splits easily into two or more
strips; combinations of mixed pastels ripped into
long skinny curlicues and dangling every which
way from a bouquet are like giggles and laughter.
I use leftover curlicues as "grass" in small baskets
of cut flowers to give at Easter and save all the

SPRING STORM

A blizzard of pink petals flying
from the cherry plum tree
carpets the garden with scented snow.

scraps to line nests for small gift plants tied with matching ribbons.

Other trimming ideas: a strip of lace tied in a soft bow, or a bow crisped with iron-on starch; a lacy handkerchief bunched in a ruff around the neck of a bouquet and tied with matching satin streamers; lace doilies, crocheted antimacassars, colorful napkins.

Here are ways we used ribbons at Okeden:

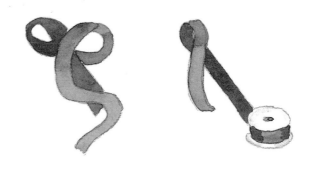

BRANCHES AND BOWS

· The earliest flowers for giving at Okeden were great bunches of fragrant yellow daffodils. They were beautiful combined with curved whips of golden forsythia and tied with masses of split yellow curling ribbon.

· Once we had only one stem of coral-pink flowering quince to give away, but it looked like so much more tied with a huge floppy bow made from a wide strip of sheer silk crepe in a soft apricot-pink.

· Another time we taped together two bud-studded branches of flowering quince with silvery pussy willows, a few big yellow daffodils, blue-purple irises, and huge yellow tulips. We covered the tape with a wide, soft silk ribbon in a blue-purple shade.

· When apple blossoms came into bloom while a few red-flecked white peonies were still available, we tied them together with a wide crimson-purple satin bow and cut the ends the length of the stems.

FLOWERS AND RIBBONS

· We tied nosegays of sweetly fragrant woodland violets with many lengths of narrow satin ribbon in shades of violet, purple, palest pink, and cream. Streamers of the ribbons floated beyond the stems, knotted at the ends.

· In May for the parlor, we bought bouquets of fragrant sweet peas in glorious pastels and tied braided quarter-inch ribbons in matching pastels around the vases.

· One year in June the garden gave us an extraordinary harvest of white foxglove, probably 'Alba', which we combined with asparagus fern harvested from an overgrown houseplant. We set the bouquet in a three-foot-tall fluted Victorian floor vase and tied around the neck a huge soft bow made from delicately patterned white and green silk print.

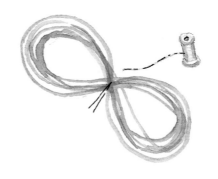

· In early summer, we added two-foot stems of deep purple-blue Siberian irises to all our mixed bouquets and focused on the color by tying them with matching taffeta ribbon.

BEAUTY SPOT

Under a bough of the green cedar tree,
sphinxlike,
the green-eyed cat in black mink fur
contemplates
five red tulips on tall green stems.

6

Wildflowers Came First

WE LOVED THE WILD FLOWERING of the landscape at Okeden and hungered for more — for Eden, nature's own untrammeled robust planting. For complex, rather cynical reasons of his own, Marrow Chapman helped us find it.

During those years, Marrow acted as handyman for Okeden and other "hill toppers," as the townspeople called the refugees from Gotham. Marrow was the last of a long line of Sharon dairy farmers. He and his schoolteacher wife had no children and eventually could find no farmhands to hire. Marrow sold the farm and built a ranch house in a woodsy lot at the end of Main Street, where the mansions thin out. Then he had nothing to do, and gradually he seeped into our lives as handyman and keeper of Sharon wisdom.

FOR LOVE OF
WILD ASTERS

Marrow was as lean as a cowboy and had hard, gnarled hands as strong as the hands of my French peasant cousins. A weathered brown fedora sat back from his forehead, and a little graying fair hair showed here and there. When I came out to dance ecstatically around Okeden's uninhibited growth, he'd stop and lean on his spading fork, not charmed.

"It's just plain ruined and going back to wilderness," he'd say, and spit sideways. "Woods were that thick hereabouts, and it took a family a whole summer to clear one acre."

Marrow brooded till August; then one day he kicked the stand of wild asters I was harvesting, and said, "You really like these weeds?"

"Yes, I really do!" I said.

"You'd like them even if they were all over everything?"

"Yes, I would."

"Then you go on up West Woods Road to my wood lot," Marrow said, in a grand-slam voice, "and we'll see who laughs last."

If you head west on Main Street, then swerve to the left where Main forks right, you'll be on West Woods Road. About a mile farther, it takes a sharp left around the farmhouse fronted with smoke trees, crosses a little stream, and begins the climb up Sharon Mountain. The stretch called Chimney Hill used to be your basic goat track, one lane studded with bare rock that grabs the muffler, and dense forest and underbrush on either side. At the top of Chimney Hill the land levels out briefly. On the left was Marrow's forty-acre wood lot.

We first saw it on a warm fall day. With the scent of hemlocks and ferns all around, we explored the roadsides and the woods, gathering wild grasses, goldenrod, milkweed, purple asters, Queen Anne's lace, and joe-pye weed. At the entrance to the wood lot, a baby swamp maple had colored the prettiest red-pink I'd ever seen. The sheer rock wall rising behind had been terraced by nature, and long ago wagons had traveled a broad stony ledge zigzagging to Mile Rock at the top. On the way to the zigzag road we found a wash carpeted with maidenhair ferns running the length of a mound shaded by young hemlocks and sugar maples.

"The garden would be here in the wash," a voice inside me whispered.

When spring came, Marrow dared us to climb to Mile Rock. It was sweaty going and barren once we got there, but the way up was forested with wild mountain laurel blooming pink. We looked down on moss-green hemlocks and the tossing tops of leggy shadblow, which were covered with dainty white blossoms. We saw a cardinal and its mate, and as we drove home, a flock of goldfinches crossed the road from a wild apple tree on the left to a slope covered with barberry in winter crimsons. In the muddy shoulder of the road just at the foot of Chimney Hill we found gold, a stretch of marsh marigold in bloom. The blossoms are like fat buttercups, gold satin, with gold anthers and luscious bright green leaves. Kris located a satisfying clump with one or two already open, and a dozen round buds. Barefoot, mud squishing cool and soft around our toes, we dug them with our hands while David and the Weensies drove back to Okeden to fetch the empty goldfish tank. We eased the plants into the tank and used a paper cup to fill it a quarter full of brown ditch water. With a worm or two and some water bugs, the flowers flourished in the tank for ten days or so. After the last bud had dropped, we drove the little kingdom back and replanted it. Woodsy soil, moss, and low-growing plants that bore minuscule bluish blossoms replaced the marigolds in the tank; hepatica, perhaps? They were followed by a family of woodland violets.

Since we couldn't move all the wildflowers into Okeden with us, we persuaded Marrow to sell us the land. Then we cleared it and built a home appropriate for a woodland — an adaptation of an Elizabethan half-timber house. With real satisfaction, Marrow helped us to cut down trees and burn the brush. But when he realized that we would clear only as much as we really needed for the house, he decided we were crazy. He told us Mrs. Chapman had said real Elizabethans would have cleaned it *all* up. How else can you see the wolves that lurk and who's coming up the drive? Also, it gets rid of the bugs.

"What bugs?" I hadn't noticed bugs.

In the language of flowers, mountain laurel means "ambition."

THE REVENGE OF MARROW CHAPMAN

M ARROW Chapman had his revenge on the city slickers who wanted to reinstate the wilderness that generations of Chapmans had fought. By the time our house on Chimney Hill was habitable, it had disappeared into the woods. Or you could say that the landscape soon looked much the way it did when God put it there. We considered naming it Eden Achieved.

The area we had cleared went native in spring with all its heart and soul. The tall maples and shadblow and hemlocks in just one season had filled in all the air space we had cleared. Vines flourished and underbrush came back head-high for having had a touch of direct sun. Two immensely tall white birches so dominated the front yard that the new grass took sick. Eventually, snowmelt made a pool at the mouth of the wash, drowning the irises and providing a hatchery for mosquitoes so numerous the spring peepers couldn't keep up. We forgave them for the sake of their sweet night keening, which promised good weather that we hoped might dry the pool. But warmth didn't dry the pool. Our house blocked the water's exit downhill. We spent that month's recreation allowance on a sump pump to dry the basement.

My mother-in-law had given us Rembrandt tulips in the fall — they were legal in those days — and said, "Put these in now." That was my first inkling that for this property, the main gardening tool was going to be a pickax. There probably are forests where "humus from the woods" is loose and three feet deep — woodsy loam, that glorious soil conditioner garden writers recommend — but they are not part of my experience. The trees at Chimney Hill had started out on naked rock, so they'd had only a few eons to develop humus. As soon as the microbial families went to work returning fallen leaves to their primal mineral elements, wiry feeder roots from the trees and shrubs invaded the soil and digested everything. Our earth resembled a horsehair mattress.

There was nowhere to get my hands into the dirt.

Then there were the bugs. When we first climbed Chimney Hill, the major bug seasons had come and gone, and stragglers had been eaten by the birds that retreat to the deep woods in hot months. But in spring, the insects come alive, a full ecological complement accompanied by that deadly triangular bomber known as the deer fly. One bite leaves your face looking as though you had lost a boxing match. Mosquitoes are the reason screened porches are added to all houses in Connecticut. Marrow said, "Wear a hat. They won't bite." He allowed himself to laugh.

He also said, "There were no deer flies on our farm because we cleared away the woods and didn't let 'em back."

I couldn't garden because of the soil, and I couldn't work on the soil because of the bugs. Instead, I spent my gardening time at the windows, designing gardens in my head, and at the typewriter, writing my first book about gardening. When we left Chimney Hill, gardens for that wooded hillside were still only in my mind. I hold no regrets. Chimney Hill is a beautiful, enduring house, and all the flowers it needs will come to it as they came over the years to Okeden. But I must acknowledge Marrow's wisdom: sometimes it is necessary that trees be cut, underbrush cleared. Still, that rocky wooded hill with its mosses and its mountain laurels changed us all. It gave our family a glimpse of gardens that bloom without us, to please only their creator.

FLOWERS EVERY DAY

A friend who spent many weekends with us in Sharon bought a little yellow house in the valley west of Sharon, and in early spring had its meadow tilled an inch deep to make a place for wildflowers. We took the children and a picnic, and fluttered over the field broadcasting sand mixed with wildflower seeds. We patted the seeds down with our hands and did a rain dance on them in bare feet. Then we ate our picnic in the setting sun by the stream that runs down the middle of the valley, waiting for rain.

The plants came up, and many weeks later the meadow bloomed. We worked a whole afternoon making a garland of greens, grasses, and wildflowers intended as the first strand of a Maypole. By dark we decided it must take a whole village working all day to make a Maypole. So we cut our garland into bracelets and crowns and danced around each other instead of a Maypole. The crowns dried on the mantel at Chimney Hill, smelling faintly of clover and hay long after the wildflowers in the meadow had set seed and been given their first annual mowing.

WILDFLOWER
GARLANDS
AND WREATHS

Garlands, crowns, wreaths, and similar floral decorations are made by wiring sprigs of greens, grasses, and flowers to a base.

Materials

· Garlands, crowns, bracelets, and other trailing creations are based on what florists call a lead wire — heavy gauge wire (22-gauge) or rope — cut to the length the garland is to be. Wire will hold the shape you give it; rope is more flexible.

· The base is covered with wild or cultivated floral materials cut into sprigs five or six inches long:

background greens such as privet, boxwood, asparagus fern, ivy, vinca, lemon leaf;

decorative leaves such as magnolia, holly with berries, laurel leaves, herbs;

flowers and other ornaments such as pine cones and bows.

· The stems of these materials are wired onto the base with 24- or 26-gauge wire. Some are wired individually first:

short-stemmed leaves and flowers;

special items such as pine cones and bows.

· Stems too fine for wiring or insertion, and clusters of small flowers, are secured with flower picks.

Basic Steps

· Cut the lead wire to desired length.

· Gather and prepare all the plant materials.

· Fasten four to six sprigs of background greens at one end of the lead wire, creating a thickness of two to three inches. If the garland is to lie flat — as on a table top or a bracelet — keep the fullness to the top. If it is to hang, like a mantelpiece garland or a bell pull, keep it full all around. *All* the stems must point in the same direction. Bind them firmly around the lead wire with the fine-gauge wire. Don't cut the wire.

· Wire flowers, leaves, and other decorative materials onto the base;

make sure you have enough of them to spread the whole length of the garland.

· Make the next group of background greens as close in fullness to the first group as possible, and arrange them so they hide the stems above. Bind these into place, then more flowers.

· Continue until you are nearing the end of the lead wire. Place the last two sets of greens pointing backward, and bind in extra greens to finish, with all stems hidden.

Wildflower Garland

Wrap the wire in background greens, as above. Then wire on wildfowers. Dryish flowers stay fresh longer. When gathering plant material, cut the flowers last and keep them in water. Some flowers that last and retain much of their color as they dry are asters, clover, daisies, coreopsis, Queen Anne's lace, purple coneflower, gaillardia, black-eyed Susans, goldenrod.

Garland of Wild Grasses

Combine short bundles of grasses, their flowering stalks, and masses of field daisies. This garland smells especially nice when it dries if you include some of the fragrant herbs once used for strewing — hyssop, meadowsweet, woodruff, rosemary, thyme, lavender, yarrow.

Crown of Flowers

A crown is fuller than a garland and includes more flowers.

• Gather and prepare lots of daisies, butter-and-eggs, Indian paintbrush, and other colorful flowers from the meadows and roadsides. A few garden flowers will finish the crown nicely — purple statice, dogwood, feverfew, sprays of forget-me-not, ageratum, calendula, sprigs of gold or pink achillea, blue hydrangea. Use a flower pick to bind in fresh bay leaves, mountain laurel leaves, or andromeda. Add silvery accents — sage, artemisia, lamb's-ears, sprigs of sedum, and sedum flowers — anything gray that grows wild.

• Cut the lead wire so that two inches will remain at each end to bind the crown into a circlet.

• Distribute the prepared plant materials along the lead wire before you wire them on. Space noticeably different colors — silver, for instance — evenly around the crown. Keep your best flowers at the front center.

• Pack the plant materials more fully than for a garland.

Daisy Chain Bracelet

• Gather an armful of field daisies, and soak them in water containing floral preservative. Cut the flower stems five inches long, wire a dozen or so, and keep them in water.

• For background greens, prepare half a dozen tip ends of evergreens such as laurel, andromeda, or ferns, and clusters of Queen Anne's lace, baby's-breath, or forget-me-nots.

· Cut a lead wire the circumference of the wrist, plus two inches at each end for closing.

· Distribute the plant materials around the lead wire, and wire them on. When the chain is complete, twist the wired daisies so they face up.

Laurel and Wildflower Wreath

· For the base, gather whips of, for instance, wild grape, young birch, willow, or honeysuckle. Strip away protruding foliage and twigs, and bind the whips together to make a double or triple circlet.

· Gather one or two long, pliable stems from plants such as honeysuckle, ivy, grape, eucalyptus, passionflower, confederate jasmine, or Japanese maple, and wind them through the wreath.

· Gather, prepare, and wire wildflowers onto the wreath — clover, buttercups, daisies, Queen Anne's lace, black-eyed Susans, gaillardia, prairie coneflower, rock cress, goldenrod, asters.

· Wire individual laurel leaves, fresh or dried, and affix them to the wreath.

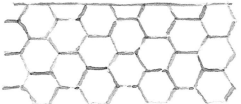

A FLORIST'S TOOLS

Making flowery things is more fun than buying them if you have patience and a modest supply of the tools of the trade. You'll find them in various places — florist shops, florist's supply centers, craft shops, five-and-dime stores, some hardware centers. This small list covers the most useful things:

· Oasis, a foam base for flower arrangements.

· Florist's wire, in gauges 22 (heavy), 24, 26, and 28 (fine), for wiring flowers, wreaths, potpourris, swags, everything.

· Forms, for wreaths and topiary trees.

· Sphagnum moss, for lining baskets and stuffing hollow wire forms.

· Sheets of green moss, to finish off low arrangements.

· Flower vials, for individual stems of fresh flowers.

· Flower picks, for delicate stems, fresh or dried.

· Silica gel, for drying flowers.

· Flower spike and adhesive clay, to anchor Oasis.

· Fine chicken wire, to hold unanchored Oasis in a bowl.

· White spray paint, to color branches and baskets.

7

Roses

SOME FLOWERS HAVE the power to draw you into a relationship whether you want it or not. I had never wanted to grow roses because I don't like dealing with black spot and Japanese beetles.

My affair began when a well-meaning friend pointed out a lonesome rose by the supermarket checkout counter. It was corseted in a ragged cardboard container, five branches sticking up like a drowning hand with a few wilting leaves attached. Under a garish picture of a pink and yellow hybrid tea was the label 'Chicago Peace'. All the other roses had been sold. My friend said, "We can't leave it here to die."

She was right; I couldn't. We popped it into the cart and later planted it with our blessings and lots of fertilizer beside a honeysuckle in what I then considered to be a sunny space.

BEWARE
THE RESONANCE
OF ROSES

In the language of flowers,
the rose means
"love."

The summer heat came on strong, and since even ever-blooming roses don't do much in heat, that first season I didn't expect much or worry about the light. The following spring, I fertilized 'Chicago Peace' very early and was rewarded by three extraordinary roses, sweetly perfumed. The first one seemed the size of a small grapefruit by the time it was half open, pink with pale lemon at the base. Since cold weather still threatened, I cut the flower and put it into a bud vase set in a silver bowl. It opened, and opened, for days. We were awed. The next two roses that I cut unfolded in the same astonishing way, but each was smaller than the previous one. Then the spectacular beginning was over. The next roses were ordinary. That summer I watered and fertilized my roses, and the honeysuckle grew, arched, joyously filled out, and soon provided enough shade to keep the rose from ever blooming again.

That same summer, a baby elm shading the fence we shared with the uphill neighbor was devoured by messy worms, and the neighbor cut it down. Hot sun burst in. Before my head knew what my hands were doing, I was digging a deep bed in this patch of sun. Planting holes for roses must be deep because the roots are long, straight, and rigid, and they need to hang straight down over a mound in the hole. All the ground-up leaves and compost we had went into this bed. The small, sunny space — about four feet by four feet — had room for three bushes. The bed was intended for 'Chicago Peace', but it needed two more roses to look full. I ordered a fragrant yellow named 'Golden Showers' and a long-stemmed hybrid tea rose called 'Sheer Bliss' — an exquisite cream-blushed-shell-pink with an irresistible name.

By midspring the new roses were planted, but I was too involved with deadlines to move 'Chicago Peace', the rose that started all this. 'Chicago' put out a whole complement of leaves and stopped everything when the sun-blocking honeysuckle leafed out. I abandoned my urgent deadline and transplanted 'Chicago'. It shed all its leaves and for weeks sat there and did nothing. I fertilized every two weeks, watered once a week if we were without rain, and prayed. After a long, cool, rainy spell, 'Chicago Peace' budded, leafed out, and by golly, bloomed! The flowers were not amazing, but nice.

'Sheer Bliss' then shot out a long stalk and opened beautiful, rich green leaves edged with a line of maroon red. Then came four long, elegant buds. When I picked one, it opened, but it gave little scent and faded quickly in the heat. The purple salvias, young lavenders, and the edging of chrysanthemums bushed out. 'Golden Showers' produced two small roses. Another blossom came from 'Chicago Peace'. The heat worsened, and the roses shut down. In high heat you don't water much, or fertilize, or prune, or harvest, or do anything else that stimulates growth.

Fall came. The roses began to grow again, and their leaves turned bright green. Indian summer slipped in and lingered. One day I saw that three buds had begun to swell on the top branch of 'Sheer

Bliss'. The leader grew larger and larger, until it was at least three inches long and elegantly oval. Frost threatened. I sat on the back steps. To cut or not to cut was the question.

I cut. There followed one of those fall storms that lash the trees and shred blossoms. In its vase indoors, 'Sheer Bliss' opened out in a seemingly endless unfolding of shell-pink petals, shading to rose at the outer edges as they matured. It looked more like a lotus than a rose. My 'Sheer Bliss' bud was pampered, of course. At night I moved the vase to a cool, dark room. I cut the stem under water and changed the water every day. It lasted a very long time — I don't remember the exact number of days. The swelling, and then the unfolding of the petals and our delight are what we remember. The perfume changed as the rose opened, too. At first the scent was light, and then there were richer undertones. Even if I imagined them, the memory of the experience is what counts.

When 'Sheer Bliss' finally dropped first one petal, then another, I drew them in around the base of the vase to dry, and eventually they went into my potpourri jar. That had been one of Mama's rituals. Mama kept a potpourri doll in a corner cabinet with glass shelves and a curved glass door. The doll was dressed in a pale pink silk gown and reclined on a matching silk chaise longue. Her shelf was covered with the dried petals of fragrant roses. Some rose petals, such as 'Golden Showers', are quite fragrant even after they dry. When Mama opened the cabinet to take out her little statue of Saint Francis, I'd catch a scent, dry like ancient silk, sweet, haunting.

Now I understand why the rose — a favorite of Japanese beetles, disease, and aphids, and anything but carefree to grow — is the most popular flower in American gardens and our national flower. Roses are the magical blossoms that I will never take for granted, the ones I will find sun and time for. The air is so sweet when I'm working in the rose bed, any excuse will do to be there with them.

GRAND OLD PERFUME ROSES

THE sweetly fragrant Old Garden Roses (the official classification for antiques) bloom mostly in spring. They will thrive in big tubs on a porch or terrace if given at least six hours of sun a day. They require care, but the sense of history that these older forms bring stops the clock if you catch them at just the right moment of early morning. It's as if you are with Josephine at Malmaison. Some have fabulous perfume.

White Rose of York

Rosa x *alba* 'Celestial', four to five feet tall, bears very fragrant, delicate, blush pink blooms. Nice rose hips.

Bourbon Rose

Rosa x *borboniana* 'La Reine Victoria', five to six feet tall, was introduced in 1872. It bears richly fragrant, cupped, medium-pink blooms in spring. Repeats occasionally.

Cabbage Rose

Rosa centifolia 'Fantin Latour', five feet tall, bears many fragrant, very double blooms. A favorite of the great Dutch painters.

Crested Rose, Chapeau de Napoleon

Rosa centifolia 'Cristata', up to six feet tall, has a mossy covering and is dark pink, very fragrant, very double.

Damask Rose

Rosa damascena, 5 to 5½ feet tall, was grown in ancient Rome. Its gift is fragrant clusters of huge, flattish blossoms with a quartered effect, in white, pale pink, or red. 'Madame Hardy' is one of the most beautiful white roses.

Harison's Yellow

Rosa x *harisonii* has arching canes five to seven feet tall and bears very fragrant, semidouble, deep golden yellow roses. Naturalized on the frontier, it may be the inspiration for "The Yellow Rose of Texas."

Apothecary Rose

Rosa gallica 'Officinalis', up to five feet tall, is an extremely fragrant rose grown commercially near Provins, France, in the eighteenth century. The petals are more fragrant after drying. Avoid this one where mildew is a problem.

NOSEGAYS

The literal meaning of *nosegay* is "something pretty to smell." In summer's high heat, big bouquets of roses are quick to fade. Little nosegays last longer. Late in the afternoon, I cut a couple of just-opening roses and cure them in a large container of cool water out of the sun. Then I gather a few pretty things from the garden and arrange them in a small vase filled with lukewarm water. I recut the stems under water before arranging them.

 # FLOWERS EVERY DAY

POTPOURRIS AND ROSE BOWLS

THROUGH the ages the fragrant varieties of roses have been a main ingredient of dry perfumes. Our drying methods haven't changed much. This recipe, To Dry Roses for Sweet Powder, was published in 1682 in *Mary Doggett: Her Book of Recipes.*

> Take your Roses after they have layen 2 or 3 days on a Table, then put them into a dish and sett them on a chafering dish of Charcole, keeping them stirred, and as you stir them strew in some powder of orris, and when you see them pretty dry put them in a gally pot till you use them.

To prepare rose petals for a modern potpourri, we still spread them over screens in a dark, warm room until they dry to a leathery state. Complete the drying in an oven heated to the lowest setting. Keep the oven light on and check every thirty or forty seconds — the petals will yellow if they dry too long.

To retain the fragrance in potpourris and dry perfumes, we still use orris root powder and other fixatives. Orris powder is the ground root of *Acorus calamus,* sweet flag. An irislike native of marshy places, this ancient fragrance herb has a sweet lemony scent. It is available at pharmacies and specialty shops like Caswell-Massey shops, Kiehl's, and Aphrodisia in Manhattan, along with other potpourri ingredients, such as dried rose and lavender buds, gum benzoin, and oil of styrax. Keep potpourris closed except when in use, and renew them often with essential oils.

You can dry a whole bouquet of roses. Cut buds that are just

BASKET OF ROSES

Clean a rustic basket, and spray it white with a matte-finish paint from a craft shop or notions store. Line the basket with a plastic container holding an inch or two of water. Pack as many buds of pink sweetheart roses as you can into the basket — two dozen or more — and tuck in among them sprigs of silvery dusty miller and baby's-breath. Cover the edges with damp green moss. When the water runs out, the roses will dry.

opening on long stems at the hottest, driest moment of the day. Bind them loosely together and hang them upside down to dry in a cool, dark, well-ventilated place.

Easy Rose Potpourri

3 cups dried rosebuds or petals
½ teaspoon coarsely ground cloves
½ teaspoon coarsely ground cinnamon
1 teaspoon dried mint leaves

½ teaspoon coarsely ground allspice
1 ½ teaspoons orris root powder
3 drops of oil of roses

Combine the rosebuds, spices, and mint in a small bowl. Mix in the orris root powder, and the oil of roses. Seal into a jar, and cure in a warm, dry place for six weeks, shaking gently every day. Transfer the mixture to small potpourri containers or to a single large bowl with a lid.

Rose Potpourri with Coriander

Freshly ground coriander has a sweet, spicy aroma and combines with the other ingredients in a delicate but exotic scent. Add more of the fragrant oils if you wish.

6 cups dried rose petals
6 cups dried pinks or wallflowers
1 ½ cups orris root powder
2 tablespoons freshly ground cloves

1 cup dried coriander
3 drops oil of roses
1 ounce gum benzoin or oil of styrax

Combine all the dry ingredients in a bowl. Stirring constantly, add the oils a drop at a time. Seal in a container, and cure in a dry, warm place for six weeks, shaking daily.

Rose Bowl with Lavender

Ground tonka beans have a sweet aroma, like vanilla, and add a sustaining note to the fragrance of this mixture. The rose leaves bring in a tender faded green.

8 cups of fragrant rose petals
4 cups small dried rose leaves
6 cups dried lavender buds
⅔ cup orris root powder
4 tablespoons coarsely ground
    allspice

4 tablespoons coarsely ground
    cinnamon
¼ cup coarsely ground cloves
4 tonka beans, ground
4 drops oil of roses
2 drops oil of lavender

Combine all the dry ingredients in a bowl, and mix in the oils a drop at a time. Seal the mixture into a jar, and cure it for six weeks in a dry, warm place, shaking daily.

Old English Rose Bowl

7 cups fragrant dried rose petals
1 cup dried rosebuds
½ cup dried rose geranium leaves
1 ounce sandalwood shavings
2 cups orris root powder

⅛ ounce oil of roses
½ ounce oil of bergamot
½ ounce oil of musk
⅛ ounce oil of sandalwood

In a large bowl, mix the dried roses, geranium leaves, and sandalwood shavings with the orris root powder. Stirring constantly, add the perfume oils a few drops at a time. Seal into jars and allow to cure in a dry, warm room for six weeks. Shake the containers daily to blend the oils.

Rose Bath Cologne

½ cup fresh fragrant rose petals
½ cup 70-proof alcohol
2 tablespoons thin lemon peel
1 tablespoon thin orange peel

1 tablespoon dried basil
1 tablespoon dried peppermint
1 cup boiling water

Soak the rose petals in alcohol for six days in a tightly closed jar. On the fifth day, steep the lemon, orange rind, and the herbs in the boiling water. Cover, and let stand overnight. Strain the liquid until clear. Drain the alcohol from the rose petals. Combine the water and alcohol in a jar and cover tightly. Shake well before using.

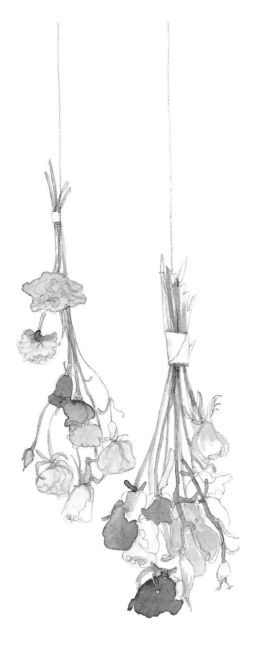

8

Lessons in Love

Many annuals require pinching. In his heyday, Papa Chéri was a world-class pincher, and wherever he was, there were always flowers. Late one summer in the dreary 1930s, some years after my parents' first separation, Papa Chéri left his failing food-importing business in Paris and came to Ottawa to support us. People worked Saturday mornings then, including Papa, who was foreman of a construction crew building a bridge across the Ottawa River. Late Saturday afternoons at the open-air farmers' market, Papa could buy both a dozen gladiolas and a big sack of potatoes for a dollar. On the way to the market, he passed the flower planters of Château Laurier Hotel, and he'd pinch seeds from the crimson four-o'clocks as he went by. When he got home, he'd run up the stairs

two at a time, gladiolas and potatoes swinging, and call to Mama: *"Touffée! Touffée!"*

After Papa had dumped the vegetables in the kitchen, he'd take the four-o'clock seeds from his pocket and hold them out to me to sort ripe ones from green ones. Ripe seeds are sooty black and fall out of the sepals. We collected them in a jar stored in the refrigerator. In the spring, Papa dug a planting bed around the edge of the grass in front of our building and showed me how to plant seeds just under the surface. That summer the four-o'clocks scented our sundowns, and I harvested seeds from our own plants.

Wherever we went, Papa Chéri found flowers. And food. That year, the last before he went off to help save France from Hitler, September was warm. I wasn't due back in the convent until late in the month, so the three of us drove around the Gaspé Peninsula. We boarded with farmers, and some mornings they'd take us out onto the St. Lawrence River in their fishing boats. It was a lazy time of year. The crops were in, and my parents were good fishermen. By noon we'd be back at the dock with a dozen thirty- to sixty-pound cods. The cod is a big, lazy gray fish that sits on your line, still as a stone. The farmers filleted the catch and racked extras in the sun to dry for salting. As a first course, the farm wives served crisp, golden, butter-fried cod tongues and cod liver, which are delicacies of the region.

Coming from a fishing village, Papa loved to fish and forage. As soon as our night's lodging was settled, he'd borrow a pail and swing down to the stony St. Lawrence beaches to see what he could find. Once he brought back periwinkles. He cleaned the small snails with infinite patience and poached them with herbs. They were served in bowls with garlic-parsley sauce accompanied by a platter of bread, still warm from the outdoor clay ovens, and freshly churned butter. Papa gave us bent safety pins with which to remove the *bigorneaux* from their shells. Another time Papa came back from the shore with about a dozen salty little oysters. He opened them with his pocketknife and gave them all to us, leaving not even one for himself. His excuse was that if he had one, he'd have to have four dozen. He loved to spoil us. Often, Papa found huge colonies of shiny black mussels. The farmers believed they were poisonous. Papa steamed them with garlic and white wine, and oh, they were so good!

Always, Papa found flowers. In late summer and early fall the ditches in eastern Canada are full of daisies and goldenrod. But I also must say that my father never met *Lychnis coronaria* that he didn't want to transplant, nor a rose he wasn't willing to pinch. When I was divorced and working in Manhattan, the children spent summers with Grandpère and Grandmère on Cape Cod. I'd come for the Fourth of July and again in September to shut down the house. Papa Chéri would drop us off at our friend Sally's and leave muttering about wild mushrooms in the schoolyard. He'd come back with a clutch of small pink roses. Probably 'The Fairy', which grew on a fence several blocks away. When Sally arched her eye-

brows, Papa shrugged and said, *"Je les ai pincées, c'est tout."* He'd simply helped to deadhead the roses, though a bit prematurely.

Papa Chéri was a very good garden pincher in other ways, too. He taught me to pinch out the suckers between tomato branches and to get tomatoes setting early by nipping off the stem tips after two flower buds had opened. He showed me where to pinch the branch tips of young fruit trees and flowering shrubs in late winter to keep their shapes symmetrical and to increase branching. The more branches, the more places where flowers and fruit can set. And it was Papa who taught me to pinch out the tips of the central stems of branching flowers, especially annuals, when planting them. The pinched plants branch generously and grow stocky and sturdy, with many flower-bearing stems.

Papa Chéri also encouraged me to spend a few moments every morning out in the garden pinching out fading flowers. Deadheading in a dressing gown, coffee in hand, good music coming from the open kitchen door, puts you in touch with the important things in life. Deadheading makes plants more productive, especially pansies, petunias, roses, and any flower whose seed formation slows flowering — true for most flowers except impatiens. Impatiens bloom madly even when covered with their tiny green barrel-shaped seeds.

FLOWERS EVERY DAY

BASKETS, BARRELS, AND STRAWBERRY JARS

HANGING baskets, barrel gardens, and strawberry jars accommodate a very satisfying variety of flowers and herbs. The plantings can be as simple as a basketful of petunias, as complex as a strawberry jar herb garden, and as expansive as a barrelful of flowers, herbs, fruits, and vegetables, such as strawberries, early radishes, and cherry tomatoes.

Rich soil, sand for good drainage, lots of moisture-holding humus, and daily watering in summer make small gardens produce like big gardens. Now and then, top the containers off with good potting soil. Place energy-driven plants in full sun — six hours at least — and put shade lovers where they have protection, especially from noon sun.

Plant containers should be very full. Don't skimp! As summer goes by, replace fading plants with fresh seedlings — petunias are great fillers, and they go on into cool weather.

San Francisco Triple Tiers

The flowered-over moss baskets that bloom in the rain-blessed coastal cities of the Pacific Northwest are celebrated. A magazine assignment took me to San Francisco to write about their three-tiered version. It's a concept ideal for homes with little space for gardening because you plant all around the baskets, down as well as up.

THE BASKETS

· We made a triple tier of three sturdy wire planting baskets, twelve, fourteen, and sixteen inches in diameter, and lined them with wrung-out sheet moss.

· We used a potting mix composed of organic humus, sand, and perlite.

· To link the baskets, we used four pieces of strong chain, 5½ feet long, and attached them to the baskets with one-inch S hooks.

· To hang the baskets we screwed a 2¼-inch S hook into a wooden beam in a sunny wall. The small basket's central hook and all four chains linking the baskets were hung on the big hook.

PLANTING THE BASKETS

· We planted the small top basket first, then caught the central hook of the middle basket into the small basket's bottom wires. After planting the middle basket, we hooked the big basket into the bottom of the middle basket.

· The baskets took six dozen seedlings of flowering annuals, foliage plants, and vegetables, as well as rooted cuttings from vines, climbing indoor plants, and volunteers from the garden.

· On the sunny sides, we planted lots of pink geraniums, red and gold coleus, small French marigolds, ageratum, dwarf zinnias, blue salvia, drought-resistant portulaca, and lots of sweet alyssum.

· On the semishaded sides and bottoms of the baskets, we put in pansies, violas, johnny-jump-ups, wax begonias, dwarf impatiens, cascading blue lobelia, pink polka-dot plant, and dusty miller.

· To cascade from the tops, we used ivy geraniums, petunias, variegated vinca, small-leaved ivy, and baby plants of asparagus fern.

· On the very top we sowed radish seeds, which would be ready for harvest by the time nearby flowers needed more space, and miniature vegetables, such as the elegant little radicchio and 'Tom Thumb' heading lettuce.

Barrels and Strawberry Jars

The original strawberry jar was a barrel filled with soil and pierced with irregularly placed openings two to three inches wide, beginning about a foot above the ground. Strawberries were planted there and allowed to cascade down. Modern strawberry jars are small simulations, often made of terra-cotta. I use my thirty-inch-tall jar to grow thymes and other trailing herbs — oreg-

ano, rosemary, sage. The fine-leaved mints for desserts are grown in the top along with cascade petunias.

A barrel garden can handle a whole garden, including strawberries, leafy lettuce, herbs, and annuals.

Basket Classics

The most elegant hanging baskets are moss-lined wire cages. You can buy prefitted liners, and you can also make, and renew, basket liners using sheets of florist's sphagnum moss. Put a saucer in the bottom of each basket: it acts as a small reservoir of water. The following are among the most satisfying basket flowers:

ACHIMENES

Hybrid achimenes are superb in baskets, indoors and out. Provide an eastern exposure with noon shade. Maintain moisture, and mulch the soil with sphagnum moss.

BEGONIAS

In dappled or bright shade outdoors, four to six tuberous begonias will cover their baskets with foliage and summer-long blossoms as pretty as roses. Cane-type begonias also make handsome baskets. Great in cool, moist climates.

SWAN RIVER DAISY

Brachycome iberidifolia is not a classic, but the cascading blue flowers are easily grown. In full sun they will flower six weeks after the seeds are planted and will last through spring.

PINCHING POSIES

Posy is derived from the word *poesy,* which has the same root as the word *poetry.* A posy can be a single flower or a small bouquet. In spring my desk bouquets are made of pinched-out tips of flowers and blue ageratum harvested in the late afternoon and arranged in vasettes the size of perfume bottles. Ageratum responds to frequent pinch-pruning by bushing out and flowering liberally, and it arranges its leaves so they alone are enough to make a bouquet.

GERANIUM

Half a dozen rooted stems of ivy geranium, *Pelargonium peltatum,* growing in western sun, will cover a big basket with flowers through summer and the first frosts. I love 'Summer Showers' — they can be grown from seed — and the lacy trailing Balcon, or Alpine, geraniums that bear masses of dainty single flowers. Zonal geraniums are great basket plants, too. Sandy, rather poor soil is best: water only when dry. Deadhead often.

IMPATIENS

Drooping impatiens like the Super Elfin series branch lavishly and make good basket plants for low light. Mulch the soil with chunks of sphagnum moss.

LANTANA

Fabulous near the sea! This cascading shrubby plant blooms nonstop and has rounded or flat-topped flowerheads that color yellow to orange to rosy red. Four to six seedlings will fill a basket. Provide full sun, and pinch out early. Mature plants will tolerate drought.

LOBELIA

Cascading *Lobelia erinus* is the daintiest and most intensely blue flowering plant I know. In cool, moist regions, flowers spangle the plants from spring to midfall. In the hot summers of Washington, D.C., they disappear, but I plant them in spring anyway. Pinch the plants back after each flush of bloom.

PETUNIA

Cascade petunias need constant deadheading, but in full sun with sustained moisture, the floribunda varieties bloom all summer long and into fall. Cut the plants back in midsummer and again in late summer to keep flowers coming.

NASTURTIUM

This old-fashioned herb with fresh green foliage and brilliant, spicy, orange-yellow flowers, is fast-growing and performs best in poor, rather dry soil. Plant six or eight seeds to a basket. The aromatic Gleam series trails to thirty-six inches.

VERBENA

This fast-growing, vigorous, trailing plant produces masses of flowerheads in white, red, pink, yellow, and purple throughout summer until frost. Like lantana, which it resembles, it flourishes by the sea. In cool regions, start seeds indoors in early spring.

KEEPING THE BASKETS FULL

To keep hanging baskets lush and full, every week, for as long as seedlings are available, tuck in one new annual — a petunia, for instance. As the maturing annuals begin to fade, the new plantings will take over and keep your baskets lush until cold weather.

PART III

*F*LOWERS
in *S*UMMER

9

The Comeback Flowers

THE FINEST SUMMER GARDEN I ever tended had been planted by Sally Erath in a huge, sun-drenched rectangle terraced into a sandy ledge that overlooks Old Mill Pond in Chatham on Cape Cod. A high wall of weathered boards blocked the winds that whistle over this sandy elbow of land crooked into the Atlantic south of Boston. Evening and morning, ocean fogs and land mists replace the moisture taken by the sun. With that, and the seaweed Sally had worked into the soil for decades, we had masses of flowers even during the hot, dry summers. When we bought the property, blue lacecap hydrangeas were crowding lavender three feet high; coreopsis, achillea 'Coronation Gold', and bee balm had swamped the bird feeder. White 'Miss Lingard' phlox and dwarf golden daylilies held court all summer long.

Sally had been the food editor of a Boston newspaper and later vice president of an advertising agency. When her husband had a heart attack, he retired to their cottage on Cape Cod, planted the garden, and got thin. Sally exchanged Boston life for clerking in a sweater shop on the Cape, and she grew flowers. In spite of lots of love and good food, Mr. Erath died. Head Winds was all that remained of his estate, and the other heir begged Sally to sell. In her late fifties, without husband, career, or money, she was about to lose her home and flowers.

While she was working at the ad agency, Sally had helped catalog a client's antique toy collection. The project didn't pay, but a man called Louis Marx had made a note of her name. As Cinderella Sally sat in the cinders in Head Winds, she received a summons to New York to meet with toy king Louis Marx, who wanted help in creating a line of antiques for F.A.O. Schwarz, the toy store.

Sally's new career began at once. She told us wistfully that Head Winds was for sale, and she moved to New York. The money to buy Head Winds dropped unexpectedly into our laps. Eventually, Sally retired to Chatham, where she continued as a consultant in antique toys. Sally never lost her roses or her garden — she just tended them through us.

In spring everything happening in our gardens is blatant, out in the open. In summer, the great happenings are beyond our perception, so it seems nothing is happening at all. But the flowers drowsing under the tender touchings of the bees, rustling in the breeze, are growing up, preparing flowers for next spring and summer. As the day length wanes, seeds mature, develop protective cases, and are launched toward the earth. The cold and rain of fall and winter will prepare the hard little shells for spring's wake-up call. When the right time comes, when day length and warmth meet each seed's specific needs, the germ of life within will waken, crack open its shell, press a fine shoot down into the earth, and stretch a slim arm up into air and sunlight — preparing the garden's tomorrows.

In the language of flowers, coreopsis means "always cheerful."

 FLOWERS EVERY DAY

CLASSIC TUBS AND PLANTERS

PERENNIALS bring to the garden a diversity of textures, forms, and colors that the one-time annuals just can't supply. But the very best thing about perennials is that they draw you out to see what's happened each week — and you stay to commune with the sky and the wind. Under your very eyes, spring unfolds the quilted hostas, and the artemisias inch their way from winter green to silver-white. Then the fuzz on the lamb's-ears grows so thick you can't resist stroking it. Summer mornings sparkle in dewdrops captured overnight by the crinkled leaves of lady's-mantle. And no matter how miserably hot and dry the summer is, sedum changes its spring jade for pink and lavender, then raspberry, and finally the maroon that looks so good in autumn. Liriope, lilies, daylilies, and the ornamental grasses flow and dance in the late season winds; none are more handsome than miscanthus after the flower stalks rise.

Any of these little miracles can take place in a tub or a big planter, just as they do in a garden. If their containers are big enough to buffer winter cold, perennials of all sorts and sizes can thrive for years.

• In Zones 6 and 7 a container safe for bulbs and hardy perennials has a minimum height and width of fourteen to sixteen inches. In colder zones, a few inches more is wise.

• For big containers, a mixture that is half potting soil and half soilless potting mix will lighten the weight. Add sand for good drainage, and humus to hold moisture. Top the containers with three inches of fresh soil every spring; before summer, mulch plantings with two inches of compost or mulch. In late winter, remove old stalks and scratch in a slow-release fertilizer. Add fertilizer to the water every week or so throughout the growing season.

• Air is as vital to plants as it is to us. Choose containers that have several drainage holes in the bottom and stand three inches above the deck or roof. Line containers with coarse gravel to improve drainage and aeration.

• Plan to water containers placed on hot, windy balconies and terraces every two days in spring, and daily during the hot summer weeks. Maintain moisture during fall and winter droughts. To help sustain soil moisture, garden centers offer two products horticulturists have responded to in a lukewarm way: the gel-like, water-grabbing polymers, and the new wetting agents. The gels, *if mixed very thoroughly into soil,* may increase its capacity to retain moisture. Water to which a wetting agent has been added quickly penetrates soils that tend to shed water, for instance, peaty soils and soils that have become compacted.

Tub of Fennel

Plant a big tub (or a half barrel) with high-flying green fennel, and surround it with plants like tall yellow and dwarf maroon daylilies, white daisies, clumps of bronze-leaf fennel, and white cascade petunias. The bronze-leaved fennel is like a fuzzy dill dipped in maroon dye, great for bouquets and for drying. The warm, sweet flavor enhances fish, salads, and soups.

Green fennel is the majestic *Foeniculum vulgare,* an anise-scented tender perennial, four to six feet tall, that is grown in the cooler regions as an annual. It produces a cloud of very fine leaves, and in rich soil it develops a bluish stem. The yellow-green flowers resemble Queen Anne's lace and are wonderful in the tub and in fresh or dried bouquets.

Herb Trees

Our best woody herbs are perennials that can be trained as little trees, or standards, in one growing season. The finished tree makes a pretty gift for the holidays. In early spring buy a potted herb with a straight woody stem, shrubby branching, and dainty leaves. Lavender, rosemary, and tarragon are good subjects. Hold the branches out to see if they can be pruned back to a rounded form; the initial pruning is most important in developing a tree form.

Grow the tree outdoors in sun and keep it well watered and fertilized to encourage rapid growth. Stake the central stem, and prune the head to encourage a rounded form. At each watering, rub away buds below the head, and pinch back the branches to keep the rounded form. Half the fun is musing over where to pinch when, and trying to guess and control how the plant is going to grow out.

When frost threatens, bring the plant in to your sunniest window. Water, fertilize, and pinch out unruly growth until the plant is ready to give away. Then wrap the base in lots of crisp white tissue paper and put a bow in its hair.

Geranium Tree Garden

The rather woody zonal geraniums train to standard form in about two seasons. Start the project with a full lush plant that has summered outdoors. Stake it, bring it in for the winter to a cool sunny sill, and keep the stem clear of side shoots. When branching begins after the turn of the year, pinch and prune to develop a rounded head.

For summer, transplant the tree to a sixteen-inch terra-cotta pot, and plant at its feet a small garden of variegated vinca, or ivy, and blue flowers — pansies, lobelia, Persian violets, ageratum, petunias. Continue to prune back and to encourage growth with sustained moisture and fertilizing.

Potted Lantana Tree

To train for a tree, choose weeping lantana *(L. montevidensis)*, whose drooping stems can reach a length of thirty-six inches. Start the project in early spring with a full, healthy plant that has a straight central stem. Stake the stem, and remove all stem shoots until it reaches three feet. Encourage the head to branch out by nipping the lead shoot and those that follow as soon as they form four to eight leaves. Winter the tree indoors in a cool, sunny window.

A yellow tree lantana is especially pretty in a sixteen- or eighteen-inch white plastic pot, filled at the base with masses of golden yellow flowers — creeping golden *Lysimachia nummularia,* or yellow petunias, small yellow marigolds, and gold-variegated thyme and sage.

Braided Hibiscus Tree

A braided tree looks exotic, but all it takes is suitable plants and patience. Start the project in spring with three young, pliable hibiscus, each having one fairly straight stem. Prune away the other stems, and gently but firmly work the three straight ones into a braid, then tie the braid.

If you can, give the project a head start by summering it in full sun in the ground. Stake it, and continue braiding as the lead branches grow. Remove any side shoots that form below the head. Keep the soil moist, but not soggy. Fertilize often.

In fall, hose the hibiscus down, and transplant it to a pot. Winter the plant indoors in full sun, in a room with temperatures above seventy degrees Fahrenheit. Keep the soil moist (I water mine almost daily), and fertilize monthly. If a lot of leaves drop, lack of sun and warmth may be inducing dormancy. In that case, keep the pot barely damp, and don't fertilize. When growth resumes in late winter, pinch out the longest shoots both to keep the head rounded and to stimulate growth. Repeat in early spring. Flowers will appear some weeks after the tree goes out for summer.

Plant at its feet variegated ivy or white cascade petunias and lots of matching verbena.

TOUGH LOVE

One of the surprising things I learned from
working with the horticulturists at the National
Arboretum is that stress, which slows the
growth of plants and which we tend to think of
as bad, helps produce stronger plants. That is
to say, some stress can be beneficial. Fast-
grown plants fresh from the nursery are lush as
lettuce from constant feeding and watering.
Slowly reduce both, and they will adjust to
your garden and climate, if suited to the area.

Early exposure to the stresses natural to the
neighborhood is especially important to the
future well-being of the woody plants. To
grow strong, trees, shrubs, and vines must tie
into the local soil and be shaken by winds
and weather.

10

The Once-Only Flowers

ANNUAL FLOWERS ARE the garden's fillers: instant paints, problem solvers, design savers. They splash fading spring beds, planters, window boxes, and hanging baskets with brilliant, season-long blooms. By midspring the markets are bright as Persian carpets with seedlings already showing their colors, so you can't go wrong. Like vegetables, they are once-only plants, new from seed every year. They are the easiest flowers to learn to grow, great for kids' projects. Annuals are the flowers used for bedding out.

The phrase "bedding out" describes filling and refilling garden beds with masses of flowers already in bloom. Bedding out is what kept breathtaking color in grand Victorian estate gardens like Great-Aunt Florence's place at Croyden.

BEDDING OUT WITH
GREAT-AUNT
FLORENCE

In the language of flowers,
white daisies mean
"innocence."

By the 1930s Grandmother Sadie Agnes, long a widow, had married a British diplomat and moved to London. One great side effect was that I acquired Great-Aunt Florence. Her smile, like the Queen Mother's, was serene, and my grandmother reported with admiration that Florence had never in all her life dressed herself. A substantial fortune supported her all-white wardrobe, eight cars, two chauffeurs, and downstairs staff to wait on the upstairs staff that waited on her. The staff included a very young maid whose only job was to serve tea, and six gardeners who kept four acres of flower beds in bloom.

Tea-time conversation at Croyden centered on bedding out. In fall masses of tulip and hyacinth bulbs were planted near the house and in gardens beyond. In spring, when the bulb flowers began to fade, they were replaced by sheets of bright-faced pansies and prim-roses. As they went by, in went broad bands of sweet alyssum, geraniums, lantanas, petunias, begonias, dahlias, caladiums, and in big spaces, cannas. When fall's failing light and cool air slowed the summer bedding plants, the gardeners hauled them all out and filled the spaces with potted mums.

Once I was called on the carpet for picking a peony. Great-Aunt Florence looked sad, and the gardener suggested that if I had to pick plants, I might be allowed to pick daisies in the kitchen garden. This large, square, sunny space at the back of the mansion was surrounded by red brick walls capped with stone. Broad, graveled paths separated rectangles of vegetables from the beds of flowers for cutting, and all the beds (in my memory) were edged with glisten-ing red strawberries shining up from mats of serrated bright green leaves. I picked and ate as many as I wanted. That was a lot, especially when the tea maid came out with whipped cream and powdered sugar on a silver tray.

When I'm planting annuals, I remember those strawberries and the books of stories about the famous heroes — Jason and the Argonauts, Sinbad the sailor, the Shakespearean characters — that Great-Aunt Florence sent every Christmas. I also ponder the Great-Aunt Florence bedding-out mystery. Mama heard it from the chauf-feur. When driving back to London, Mama would sit up front with him, which made Grandmother Sadie Agnes scold. Pulling her fedora over one eye, Mama would puff on her cigarette and say, "The chauffeur is the only one who thinks!"

According to Mama, Great-Aunt Florence had been a great Victorian debutante, presented at court dressed by Worth and decked with family jewels. With everyone's blessings, she fell in love with a Titled. After a splendiferous wedding sprinkled with royalty, the couple set off on a magnificently endowed honeymoon. The morning after their wedding night, the groom dressed, gave Florence a kiss, went off to breakfast — and kept going. He bedded out that night and never came back.

There were sightings by family members. Especially in midwinter, nephews and uncles would rush off to sunny Italy to check on the latest rumors of his whereabouts. But nothing concrete ever was known.

Great-Aunt Florence never stopped loving him and always wore bridal white. I asked Mama what kind of man would run away from a lady with so many flowers and strawberries. Mama said he probably was bedding out with someone who knew how to dress herself and could make her own tea.

PINK MAKES IT SNAP

I tried an all-blue flower window box once, and the blues disappeared into the greens. Helen van Pelt Wilson, my first book editor and a great garden writer, showed me the solution in her Westport, Connecticut, garden. Helen created an airy, lightly wooded area lapped by borders of both wild and domestic flowers. All Helen's blues *snapped*, which is magazine parlance for "came up off the page." The secret was pink. A few tall pink flowers brought out the pink in the blues and made them stand out from the green of the foliage.

FLOWERS EVERY DAY

**ROMANTIC
WINDOW BOXES**

WINDOW boxes are airy little gardens that give pleasure indoors and outdoors. Planted with combinations of pink, lavender, purple, and blue, with clumps of white flowers and silvery artemisia, dusty miller, or lambs'-ears, they're unabashedly romantic. Tuck in a few herbs for foliage contrast and for the fun of reaching out the window to pick parsley. When you water the window box in the morning, it's a delight to inhale basil and rub mint between your fingers.

Pack your window boxes with closely spaced plants. Water and fertilize the boxes often, but lightly, with 20-20-20. Removing plants that are crowding each other is less annoying than waiting all summer for the window boxes to fill out.

Use rich soil, and replace it completely every year. Mix in organic fertilizer, and lots of peat moss to hold moisture. In summer in a breezy place, a window box needs watering daily. The foliage growing in a successful window box tends to deflect rain. Mix a little mulch into the top layer of soil — that lets water down in, whereas a topping of mulch may deflect the water.

Floral Window Boxes

If you want to enjoy window boxes full of flowers from early spring through the summer, give your window boxes the "bedding out" treatment.

SPRING BOXES

· In the cool, damp weather of early spring, plant pansies; when the weather warms, tuck in cascade petunias of the same color. They are beautiful together, and the petunias take over as the pansies wane in the heat. Set the plants so that they are almost touching.

· Fill the box with clumps of silvery dusty miller, and garnish it with bright primroses. When the primroses go by, replace them with small orange marigolds.

· Pack the box with red, white, and blue primroses, and replant later with red geraniums, white cascade petunias, and blue ageratum edged with variegated vinca or ivy.

· Pack the box with cascading blue lobelia, and when it goes by, replant with creeping pink baby's-breath, which blooms all summer into cold weather. Interplant with dwarf cerise and pink snapdragons, and edge with pink-edged variegated ivy.

SUMMER BOXES FOR SUN

· Alternate curly parsley with fragrant white sweet alyssum. Add a few midsize zinnias in vibrant colors and clumps of dwarf snapdragons. You can harvest all three — they'll produce more.

WEEDS CAN BE WONDERFUL

When the drawers and the closet are all in order, all the wastepaper baskets are empty, all the relatives have received thank you letters, and you have run out of every possible excuse for not getting down to work, weeds are wonderful!

TENDER SECRETS

You can identify annuals sensitive to cold in your area by recalling which turn to mush with the first fall frost — impatiens, cockscomb, tomatoes, and sweet peppers come to mind. Some things that look tender are quite tough, for instance, wax begonias.

• Clump miniature dahlias in pink and yellow at the back. In front, alternate pink wax begonias and lavender-blue ageratum. Edge the box with pink Thumbellina zinnias, and cascade white petunias and variegated vinca over the edge.

• Pack the box with crisp, spicy pineapple mint. It grows upright and bears white flower spikes, and the leaves are variegated with patches of cream-white. Add masses of small white cascade petunias.

SUMMER BOXES FOR LIGHT SHADE

Plant clumps of fragrant white dwarf foxglove, fronted by impatiens in shades of hot pink, crimson, and pale pink. Edge the box with white lobelia interspersed with dwarf lady's-mantle. Lady's-mantle thrives in light shade and bears chartreuse or yellowish green flowers in late spring or early summer.

Herbal Window Boxes

In a window box even perennial herbs are grown as annuals and discarded at season's end. I've kept window boxes growing (slowly)

indoors through winter when I had available for them a cool, sunny entrance hall.

A BIG HERB BOX

My favorite mint, spearmint, does well in a window box. Ten to twenty-four inches high, it has dainty pointed leaves and sharp, refined mint flavor and an aroma that go well with both flowers and food. With it, plant four each parsley and basil plants, and a young lavender — all can be useful dried and fresh. For height add rosemary and tarragon. Plant seeds of nasturtium or marigold. Edge the box with variegated thyme, creeping thyme, and mother-of-thyme, which produces sweet, pale blue blooms in late spring.

A SMALL HERB BOX

In the center back, plant scent-leaved geraniums fronted by caraway thyme and silver variegated thyme. Behind and on either side of the geraniums, plant lavender 'Hidcote' or 'Dark Opal' basil, lamb's-ears, parsley, silver verbascum, and 'Tricolor' sage.

A VERY NARROW HERB BOX

Front the box with plants of miniature basil backed by the tiny orange marigold 'Tangerine Gem'. Anchor the bed at intervals with parsley, and center it with yellow nasturtium. Plant gold variegated thyme to drip over the edges.

Houseplants in a Window Box

Houseplants thrive on outdoor vacations, and the small pots prefer the soil of a window box to standing naked in the sun and the wind. If they've had sustained moisture and are given a good washup before they go back indoors, they'll be far more beautiful during the dark months. Among houseplants that enhance window boxes are Christmas and Easter cactuses, coleus, gardenias, Jerusalem cherries, hydrangeas, pink polka-dot plant, aloe, snake plant. The straight-up, needlelike leaves of a young dracaena make a very attractive centerpiece for a window box.

ANNUAL HAZARDS

Bedding out annuals is the key to months of constant bloom. But there are hazards. No matter how restrained I try to be, in midspring the porch is carpeted with flats of annuals I couldn't resist buying, haven't garden space for, and bought too early to plant.

Timing calls for prescience. Planted too early, the summer annuals sulk or rot. Planted too late, in high heat, they put their strength into flowering instead of growing the roots that result in full plants and masses of blooms.

11

The Perfumeries

THE MOST ROMANTIC FLOWERS are those whose perfume, vaporized by a hot May sun or rising in the crystalline chill of a spring evening, captures our senses. Today vanishes, and we are open for a moment to that mysterious, invisible, greater life that plants the forests and governs tides.

I was twenty-two when I first tried to sell my writing, and it wasn't very profitable. The old stone tenant cottage I was renting belonged to the Bertrand family farm in Mougins, a walled village in the hills behind Cannes on the French Riviera. In spring, Madame Bertrand let me pay some of the rent by helping a crew of neighborhood wives harvest jasmine for the perfume factories in Grasse. A couple of hours before dawn, we'd climb up to the

THE FRAGRANT
FIELDS OF
PROVENCE

*In the language of flowers,
sweet basil means
"good wishes."*

terraced field planted with sprawling vines where her son, Lolo, waited with harvest baskets and sacking pads. The sacking was our protection from a lot of fire ants, and a scorpion or two. Lolo assigned to each of us a long or short row of jasmine vines, according to how fast we picked. We plunked the sacking down in front of the first vine in a row, sat cross-legged, and stripped the flowers gently and quickly. They were wonderful hours, balanced between the deep, sweet awareness of the perfumed flowers and the drama of darkness fading before a relentless dawn. Now and then a woman would stand, stretch her back, gaze at the brightening horizon, and sashay up to the next row. There'd be a firecracker exchange of jokes in twangy Provençal French.

We worked fast because the vines had to be stripped before the sun was up. Heat causes the plant cells to break, vaporizing the

essential oils and reducing the yield at the perfumeries. Dew-damp blossoms weigh more; the perfumeries paid by weight.

By the time the sun was clear of the horizon, we were trooping down from the terraced hill to the farmhouse. In the big yellow-tiled kitchen, Madame Bertrand distributed bowls of sweetened *café au lait* and oven-toasted chunks of fresh baguette to dip in it. We dunked and munched, while out in the yard Lolo and his father bagged the blossoms. By the time the sacks were ready, trucks from the Grasse perfumeries were rumbling up the hill. Burly truckers jumped out, exchanged indecipherable jokes, and weighed our harvest under Lolo's watchful gaze.

At other seasons, the perfumeries bought orange blossoms and petals of fragrant old roses, particularly *Rosa centifolia,* the cabbage rose. They are the huge, multipetaled pink blossoms you see in the richly colored paintings by Dutch masters.

Walking to the Capitol Hill farmers' market Saturday mornings here in Washington, D.C., I've noticed that the men and women with glowing smiles are those with their noses close to armfuls of fresh flowers.

LATE August brings shorter days, cooler nights, greener foliage. My bare feet on the flagstones crush herbs that have overflowed their borders. Fuzzy mints, oreganos, sages, and lemon verbena have snaked past the confederate jasmine, past the Japanese anemones, vinca, and ageratum, past peonies and sedums and the wild campanula. I gather fragrant branches to combine with cosmos, pink asters, and blue salvia in the most fragrant bouquets and floral projects of the year. Most of these thrive in window boxes and planters, and this time of year, fresh cut herbs also are available at nurseries and herb farms.

HERBS AND FLOWERS FOR PERFUME

Herbs for Fragrance and Flowers

ANGELICA

Dried flowers for potpourris.

ARTEMISIA

Dried flowers and foliage, for wreaths and other projects.

BORAGE

Fresh blue flowers, for garnish and bouquets.

ENGLISH LAVENDER

All parts, fresh or dried, for scent; buds for flavor.

FERN-LEAF TANSY

Fresh foliage for scent; flowers for arrangements.

HELIOTROPE

Fresh or dried flowers for scent, potpourris, and bouquets.

HYSSOP

Leaves and flowers for potpourris.

LAVENDER COTTON

Dried flowers and foliage for scent, wreaths, and arrangements.

LEMON VERBENA

Foliage, fresh or dried, for scent.

MEADOWSWEET

Fresh or dried flowers for scent and bouquets.

MINT

Fresh or dried foliage and flowering stems, for scent and flavor.

NASTURTIUM

Fresh leaves and flowers, for flavor and garnishes.

OREGANO

Leafy tips for flavor; branches and flowers for bouquets.

PARSLEY

Fresh foliage for flavor and bouquets.

PINKS

Flowers, fresh or dried, for scent and flavor.

ROSEMARY

Leaves, fresh or dried, for flavor, potpourris; fresh or dried branches with flowers, for bouquets.

RUE

Flowers and foliage, for tussie-mussies and bouquets.

SAGE

Fresh or dried leaves for flavor; branches for bouquets.

SILVER SAGE

Flowers and foliage, fresh or dried, for wreaths and bouquets.

SWEET BASIL

Leaves fresh or dried for flavor; branches and flowers for scent.

SWEET WOODRUFF

Leaves, dried, for scent.

TARRAGON

Foliage, fresh or dried, for scent and flavor.

THYME

Fresh or dried leaves and flowers, for scent and flavoring.

YARROW

Flowers and foliage, fresh or dried, for bouquets and floral projects.

ℱLOWERS ℰVERY ᗪAY

Swag with Strewing Herbs

From antiquity through the colonial era in America, fragrant rushes and dry flowers were strewn over floors to fill the home with sweet smells (and cover the unpleasant ones). Hyssop, with its pretty flowers, was popular in England, as was sweet woodruff, which smells wonderfully of new-mown hay. Sweet woodruff was tied with stems of lavender and strewn under the pews at churches and hung up in the house, where the heat of the fire would release the scent. Yarrow was used this way, too. Elizabeth I had her floors strewn with meadowsweet, a big architectural plant with bold foliage and summer sprays of showy, sweetly scented small flowers that toss in the wind. Rosemary and thyme were counted among the strewing herbs, along with bay leaves and sweet flag — the wild iris with blue-purple flowers known to Victorians as fleur-de-lys. (The root of this variety, *Iris florentina,* is the source of orris root powder, a scented fixative for potpourris.)

· Background: lay out branches of hyssop and meadowsweet, and top them with shorter branches of strewing herbs — hyssop, meadowsweet, woodruff, rosemary, thyme, lavender. Wire them together. Do not cut the wire.

· Bind on aromatic flowers — pinks, tansy, marigolds, lavender, lilies, roses; for color, add larkspur, purple statice, daisies, clover.

· Make a wire loop at the back of the bundle with which to hang the bundle. Cut the wire.

· Use narrow satin ribbon, in lavender, gold, and rose, to hide the wire binding, and let the ends stream down.

SUMMER SWAGS

A Simple Swag

The simplest swags are made by binding together — cut end to cut end — two sturdy branches and covering them with decorative materials and a bow. For the base, use wing-shaped feathery materials — plumed cockscomb (*Celosia*), heather, cedar, juniper, privet, boxwood. Before cutting the wire binding the branches, make a hook from it at the back with which to hang the swag. Wire on garnishes, such as flowers, ornamental peppers, small fruits and vegetables.

SWAG WITH FRESH HERBS AND FLOWERS

· Lay out six stems of pussy willow or something similar, three on either side. Bind the cut ends together firmly with wire.

· Cover them with shorter branches of herbs such as white sage (*Artemisia ludoviciana*), lavender cotton, coral heather, or broom, topped by short stems of lavender, artemisia, or curry plant (*Helichrysum italicum*). Bind them all firmly.

· Wrap the wire binding in a chunk of damp moss, and wire it on. Make a wire hook at the back of the swag for hanging.

· Hide the moss by inserting in it short stems of wired yellow statice, pearly everlasting, and orange and gold flowers, such as pot marigolds, tansy, rosy everlastings, sedums, gomphrena.

· Tie streamers of narrow gold and coral satin ribbon on either side of the flowers.

LIFE AFTER LIFE

A flower that has only recently wilted often will come back to sparkling freshness if it is immersed in warm water. Let it soak, face down, for a minute or two. Under water, recut the stem end several inches from the bottom. Shake off the water, and at once place the stem in fresh, warm water to which floral preservative has been added.

SEARING EFFECT

Sear the stems of flowers that exude milk, such as euphorbias and poppies, by holding them over a flame or by giving them a quick dip in boiling water. This ends the milky flow, prevents the clogging of water-conducting cells, and helps the flowers stay fresh.

PART IV

FLOWERS in FALL

12

Of Potpourris and Stillrooms

THE FIRST GILDED AUTUMN leaves drift down to the herbs that by now are rioting among the enduring summer flowers. In moments that seem timeless, side by side with fat bees drunk on basil and mints, salvia and heliotrope, cosmos and the first late roses, we gather flowers and herbs to dry for aromatic potpourris, tussie-mussies, sachets, and the lovely old dry perfumes our grandmothers made.

In Elizabethan times and later, fragrances were also used as flavorings, and roses and lavender were stocked in the stillroom. A warm place equipped with a small still, mortars and pestles, the stillroom was perfumed by bunches of drying herbs and flowers, and shelves of spices, fixatives, and preserves. The mistress of the house

In the language of flowers,
lavender, alas, means
"distrust."

used them in her role as perfumer, candle maker, confectioner, doctor, nurse, obstetrician, cook, as well as mother and wife. Most of the information used in stillroom preparations was stored in her memory. A few recipes have come down to us in stillroom books in which the family knowledge of perfume, medicine, cooking, and gardening was recorded from generation to generation.

At the Château de l'Enardière, the gardeners planted flowers and herbs together in the gardens and in the courtyard by the kitchen door. I loved the sweetly scented days of the lavender harvest. In spring, and again in late summer, Papa and Mama would put their heads together over the lavender plants, fingering flowering stems whose buds were just showing color. The next day after breakfast we'd harvest the lavender — Rose the cook, the maids, Tante Louise, Mama, Papa, and I. Five years old, I followed my mother with a basket for the stems she snipped off close to their base with a big pair of scissors. Back in the kitchen, we spilled our gray-green harvest onto the long wooden table, and the sharp aroma quickly overpowered the familiar smells of damp tiles, wood stove, soup, bread. The women sorted the stalks, and Tante Louise tied them into loose bunches and set them in a wicker hamper. Papa carried the hamper up to the attic and hung the bunches upside down to dry on cords stretched between the rafters.

On a rainy day after they had dried, we gathered around the kitchen table to strip the buds from the stems. Small fingers can be clumsy, so I was given the stoutest lavender sticks to strip. Rose saved these sticks, and for dessert on special occasions she threaded them with raspberries or tiny, soft pastries. I remember the sound of the dried lavender buds falling into Mama's old straw hat. It was a whispery sound lost in the late afternoon to the snap of the flames in the black cook stove that Rose would light when it was time to make soup for supper. We'd break then for a *goûter* of bread and honey. (*Goûter* is the French equivalent of British family teatime.)

Tante Louise, my father's sister as well as our nanny, worked with exquisitely small, painstaking stitches to make lavender-colored net pockets edged with lace for the dried lavender buds. She decorated the sachets for Mama with small purple silk bows. I was the one who placed the sachets among the linens on the bottom shelves of the closets.

I plant lavender in the few sunny places that remain in my shady garden — by the roses, behind the kitchen herbs. Cultivating the beds, digging begonias and parsley to pot up for a winter indoors, my hands brush lavender, and I come back to the house feeling deliciously aromatic.

TUSSIE-MUSSIES are nosegays composed of flowers and herbs. Elizabeth II was handed a tussie-mussie as she entered Westminster Abbey on the day of her coronation. In earlier centuries tussie-mussies conveyed messages to lovers in a code called "the language of flowers." It was brought to the courts of Europe by Crusaders

THE LANGUAGE OF FLOWERS

returning from the Middle East. For men and women in the reign of Elizabeth I, each herb and flower had a specific meaning. Shakespeare had a fragrant garden, according to legend, and he wrote herbal lore into his plays. In *Hamlet,* after her father's death Ophelia describes a tussie-mussie that conveys a tragic, bitter message to Hamlet:

> There's rosemary, that's for remembrance;
> pray you love, remember; and there is
> pansies, that's for thoughts.
> There's fennel for you, and columbines;
> there's rue for you; and here's some for
> me; we may call it herb o'grace
> Sundays; O, you must wear your rue with a
> difference. There's a daisy; I would
> give you some violets but they withered all
> when my father died.

Fennel was a symbol for flattery and dissembling, and columbines for unchastity. Rue stood for repentance and grief; mixed with holy water it was known as "herb of grace." Daisies stood for innocence, among other things. Blue violets stood for loyalty and white for innocence.

In America, colonists tied sprigs of rosemary to wedding bouquets as a symbol of remembrance. When valentines came into fashion, a sprig of rosemary was painted on a heart and sent to the beloved. In England, gilded branches of rosemary tied with ribbons were given to wedding guests, and bridesmaids wore sprigs on their left arms as a symbol of faithfulness. The lovely little sky-blue forget-me-not was a symbol of faithfulness and remembrance. It was included in tussie-mussies for people starting a journey on February 29 — the extra day in the leap year — and remains a motif of modern Valentine cards.

LAVENDER IN YOUR LIFE

Don't try to live without lavender. All parts of the plant are used in bouquets and floral perfumes. Lavender buds are a main ingredient of potpourris and sachets, and add exotic flavor to sweets, tea, sauces, salad dressings, and fish stews. They're the secret ingredient in Herbes de Provence, that greatest of all herbal mixes.

In early spring set out container-grown plants in well-drained neutral soil. The best species for fragrance is English lavender, *Lavandula angustifolia*, which is hardy in Zones 5 to 9. 'Hidcote' has dark blue-lavender flowers that are showier, but I prefer the old-fashioned species. Oil of lavender is distilled from English lavender and from Spanish lavender, *L. stoechas*, subspecies *pedunculata*. It has showy flowers and is a good choice for a basket garden.

ℱLOWERS ℰVERY ᴅAY

DRY PERFUMES AND TUSSIE-MUSSIES

TUSSIE-MUSSIES, potpourris, sachets, and other lovely old-fashioned dry perfumes are enhanced by colorful dried herbs and flowers. Fragrant roses, aromatic lavender buds, citrus rind, and spices provide some of the scent, but the main source most often is the essential oils and fixatives sold by specialists, such as the Caswell-Massey shops. The scents in dry perfumes are easily dissipated; keep potpourri containers closed when not in use. Save some of the essential oils to renew the perfume when it fades.

Lavender-Rosemary Sachet

For each sachet:
2 tablespoons dried lavender buds   *2 tablespoons dried rosemary leaves*
10 whole cloves   *¼ teaspoon dried orange peel*

Combine all the ingredients, and spoon into a sachet bag.

1880 Herbal Sachet with Lavender

1 cup dried thyme
1 cup dried lemon thyme
1 cup dried mint
1 cup dried marjoram
2 cups dried lavender buds

2 cups dried rose heels (white base
  of petal removed)
1¼ ounces ground cloves
1¼ cups dried calamus root
Few drops of musk

Combine all the ingredients and store them in an airtight container
for a few weeks so the scents mingle and mature. Shake as before.
Divide among sachet bags of net or fine lavender silk, and tie them
with narrow lavender satin ribbon.

Spicy Potpourri

4 cups dry rose and flower petals
1 cup dry lemon verbena leaves
1 cup dry lavender buds
2 tablespoons dry herb leaves —
  rosemary, tarragon, basil,
  marjoram

2 tablespoons spices — cloves,
  cinnamon, nutmeg
1 vanilla bean, crushed
2 tablespoons grated citrus rind
2 tablespoons orris root powder
3–5 drops lavender oil

In a large bowl, combine the flower petals and herb leaves. In a
small bowl, mix everything else but the lavender oil. Add the
contents of the small bowl to the large, and very gently toss them
together until thoroughly combined. Then add the lavender oil,
drop by drop. Seal into a jar, and cure in a warm, dry place for six
weeks, shaking gently every day. Transfer the mixture to small
potpourri containers or to a single large bowl with a lid.

To Make a Tussie-mussie

BASIC STEPS

· Wire five-inch stems of lavender, small garden flowers, herbs,
and rosebuds.

· Trim the stems to a uniform length, and set this bunch as a
handle in the center of a large lace paper doily. Gather the doily up
under the flowers; ideally, it will extend about a quarter-inch beyond the flowers.

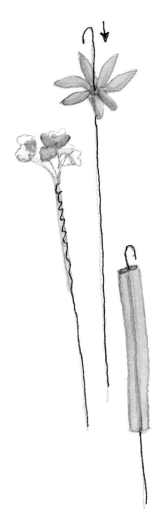

· Secure the doily with wire.

· Cover the wire with long, narrow satin ribbons matched to the colors of the flowers. Knot the ribbons in place under the flowers, and knot the ends of the streamers.

· To dry a fresh tussie-mussie, hang it upside down in a cool, airy place away from the sun for several weeks.

FRESH GERANIUM TUSSIE-MUSSIE

4 short stems of variegated sage
4 small red daisy mums
12 yellow French marigolds
6 white heliotrope

12 or more leaves of nutmeg
*   geranium*
12-inch paper doily

Gather the sage (which stands for esteem) in one hand, and circle it with the mums (meaning "I love"). Surround them with the little French marigolds (for jealousy) and then with the airy heliotrope (devotion). Finish with a row of nutmeg geranium leaves (an expected meeting). Cut the stems off evenly, set them in the doily, bring the doily up around the undersides of the flowers, secure with wire, and cover the wire with purple, lavender, and cream ribbons.

THANKSGIVING TUSSIE-MUSSIE

6 dried red zinnias
12 dried stems blue salvia
10 sprigs pearly everlasting

12 dried sprigs rosemary
12 dried sprigs garden sage
12-inch paper lace doily

Surround the zinnias (which stand for thoughts of absent friends) with the salvia (which means "I think of you"); surround them with the everlastings, then make a round of rosemary (for remembrance) and finally of sage (for esteem). Cut the stems off evenly, set them in the doily, bring the doily up around the undersides of the flowers, secure with wire, and cover the wire with long, narrow, mahogany-red ribbons.

STOCKPILE

I save baby's-breath from faded bouquets and stockpile it for use in dried arrangements. A bunch of dried baby's-breath tied with narrow, colorful satin ribbon, streamers flowing, makes a pretty wall ornament.

The easiest way to dry baby's-breath is to gather the stems together gently and cut them to equal length. Bind the stems very loosely with a rubber band, and stand the bunch in a wide-mouthed container to finish drying.

13

Foraging and Keeping

AFTER THE HARVESTERS clear the fields in late summer, wild-flowers grow up in the hedge rows, mustard comes back, and the sides of the highways bloom with black-eyed Susans, milkweed pods, crimson sumac, wild asters, blanketflower, and joe-pye weed. Goldenrod starts to color, and in wet places cattails sway beyond patches of lythrum and knotweed. This is the late, great show inviting you to gather and keep.

The best flowers are always on the other side of a muddy field full of shaved stubble. Go barefoot, but watch how you place your feet because the dry stalks can cut your instep. Growing up in Ottawa, I learned to stubble-walk on the outer edges of my bare feet in the fields flanking the Rideau River. Downriver where the water was

ACROSS A
MUDDY FIELD

*In the language of flowers,
red mums mean
"I love."*

warm, we'd swim at a little beach until our teeth were chattering and our lips blue, then we'd work our way back up the river's edge and catch crayfish. Sometimes we'd make a fire and roast the crayfish. They tasted awful. They also tasted awful to me years later in Sweden, where they are served with icy aqua vitae as the great summer delicacy. Potatoes packed in clay and baked in hot coals, that's something else!

We eight- and ten-year-olds, with a couple of tag-along baby brothers and sisters, stubble-walked in the fields. We foraged for buttercups, purple vetch, sumac, and red-berried honeysuckle branches. In the twilight, we'd amble home to the wrong side of the streetcar tracks in Sandy Hill. In the big back yard, we'd divide our treasures. Mama would tie my flowers into loose bundles, and I'd take them through the trapdoor up to the secret attic where we hid the silver when the bailiff came. When Papa had lived with us, he had strung ropes from wall to wall. I tied our wildflowers upside down on the ropes to dry. When we were ready to plan for Christmas, I brought them down to Mama, and we made dried flower arrangements for the vases in the front rooms. Flowers shrink as they dry, and the flower colors melt to soft earthy tones that are cozy when it's cold and white outdoors. A faint scent, a memory of a scent, clings to them.

WAXING LEAVES

MY bedroom window in Ottawa framed the lawn next door and two young sugar maples, one on either side of the path to the neighbor's front door. In October the days were bright and crisp, and the trees turned from green to gold and red. The evening sky burned an incandescent blue. Doing my homework, I'd hear rain begin, a rustling on fallen leaves at first tentative, then insistent. In the streetlights the maples shone gold and crimson, and the wet tree trunks were velvety black.

Mama and I waxed the most beautiful of the red maple leaves we collected and gave them as bookmarks and souvenirs. We had a small white enamel pot that Mama and Grandmother Sadie Agnes

had used for waxing leaves. Some of the enamel had chipped and that made it friendlier, like an old comforter or a worn rocker. On the smallest burner of the electric stove we heated ordinary paraffin, the kind for sealing canned foods. The only tricky part was that if we let it get too hot, the paraffin would catch fire.

When the wax had become completely liquid, we'd pick up a leaf by the stem and swish it around in the pot until it was completely coated. Then we swooped it up through the air and over to the baking sheet to cool. The wax was set by the time it landed. Later, we dipped the stem tips in wax to complete the sealing.

Waxed leaves are stiff and rather fragile. The paraffin cracks if you bend the leaves too far, but they hold their glowing colors for months. I don't remember what happened to the leaves. They are among those treasures that disappear into thin air, like pressed flowers.

WINTER BASIL

Fresh basil blackens when frozen. Dried basil is tasteless. But basil that is first dried and then frozen retains color and flavor. I place large, tender leaves between sheets of paper towel and microwave them on the high setting, one to two minutes according to thickness. Use as is in stews, sauces, and soups; reconstitute in hot water and mince for use in salads.

 # FLOWERS EVERY DAY

WINTER ARRANGEMENTS

Drying Flowers, Herbs, and Berries

After you've moved the heliotrope, begonias, and geraniums into the house, but before that blast of wind that says "plant bulbs now," it's time to prepare winter arrangements. The flowers, branches, and berries in dried bouquets call up the woodsy smell of autumn leaves, the sweet, sharp smell of goldenrod and tangy artemisia. Mauve and plum, crimson and gold, the colors are rich and romantic. There's sweetheart pink in dried roses, valentine-blue in the hydrangeas. Bring armfuls of wild fillers to the project. They shrink so! A dried arrangement takes three times as much material as a similar fresh bouquet. Air-drying is the easiest way, but other techniques for drying have their special uses.

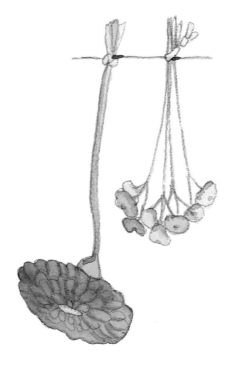

AIR-DRYING (FOR MOST ANYTHING)

· Harvest dryish materials such as the everlastings, goldenrod, knotweed, hydrangeas, and thistles just before the buds open. Gather herbs for drying on a dry day.

· Strip flowers of their leaves; thin out herb foliage.

· Make small, loose bunches, and hang them upside down in a warm, airy, dark place until they are very dry.

SILICA GEL (FOR FLOWERS)

· Silica gel, light, grainy stuff, has taken the place of clean sand as a drying agent for delicate, moist flowers. Spread gel two or three inches deep in a large box.

• Pick the flowers at peak of bloom — anemones, carnations, cosmos, zinnias, for instance — in a dry, hot moment of the day.

• Wire the flowers, and sift silica gel over and into them until they are completely covered. In gel they dry so quickly, they retain color and form. Check a test flower — in twenty-four hours if you are drying single or wild varieties. Overdried flowers shatter.

• After you take the flowers from the gel, rest them on top of it another day before storing them in tissue in labeled, airtight boxes to which you have added a few tablespoons of silica gel.

• If grains of gel cling to dried petals, brush them off gently with an artist's brush or by pouring a little clean sand over them.

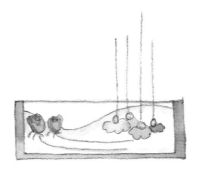

OVEN-DRYING

• An oven on low heat and a microwave oven at half power can be used to dry a few things quickly, if carefully monitored.

• Support the flower's form with a paper towel, and time a test flower. Moisture varies: a semidouble rose with twenty-five to thirty petals takes longer than a hybrid tea; an old-fashioned damask rose with up to fifty petals takes even longer. Basil leaves require 1 or 1½ minutes in the microwave, while a whole branch needs three to four minutes on high. The outside petals dry sooner than those inside. To avoid overdrying, check often on color and form through the oven window.

GLYCERIN SOLUTION (FOR LEATHERY FOLIAGE)

• Leathery foliage — euonymus, broadleaf evergreens, magnolia and holly leaves — is preserved by immersing the stems in a solution of one-third drugstore glycerin and two-thirds water. Warm the solution to eighty degrees Fahrenheit, and leave the stems in it until the top foliage darkens — from a few days to three weeks. Then air-dry them.

• Immerse trailing stems such as ivy for six days or more in a solution of half glycerin and half water.

· Baby's-breath, which also air-dries easily, is sometimes preserved by leaving the stems overnight in a solution of one part glycerin to two parts water, then hanging them upside down in loose bunches.

ALCOHOL AND SHELLAC (FOR BERRY BRANCHES)

· Berry branches are dipped in a solution of one-half wood alcohol and one-half clear shellac, then are hung upside down over newspapers to drip dry.

Shore Wreath

Foraging along the seashore and by rivers and lakes, you can find all sorts of plant materials that make good wreaths. For background greens gather blue-berried sprigs of cedar, juniper, or other evergreens. To top the greens, collect five- to six-inch stems of bright berries and late flowers — wild raspberry, cranberry, blueberry, bayberry, beach plum, grape vine; *Rosa rugosa* leaves and bright coral rose hips; Queen Anne's lace and blue asters. Chunks of moss, oak leaves in their soft fall browns, andromeda foliage taking on its winter blush, and pine cones — anything textured, scented, or colorful will enrich the mix. A double-wire wreath frame packed with damp sphagnum moss is the best base for a wreath intended for hanging outdoors.

· Cut the background greens to five or six inches.

· Wire, or secure in flower picks, pine cones and other materials whose stems are too short or too delicate to insert into the frame.

· Buy an eight- or twelve-inch double-wire frame, and two or three bags of sphagnum moss. Soak the moss in water containing floral preservative, and wring it out. Lay the frame flat, and attach to the top wire a spool of 24- or 26-gauge florist's wire. Hold a wrung-out clump of moss against the wreath wires, and wire it on. Repeat, overlapping the clumps, until the frame is stuffed and covered.

· Working up from the bottom of the wreath, on either side insert the stems of the background greens into the mossed frame until the wreath is completely covered. Place the greens so that all the stem ends are pointing to the bottom.

· Distribute berried sprigs and other showy things over the four quadrants of the wreath. Place the most colorful materials at the top and bottom, with a little extra at the bottom, and across from each other on the sides. When you are satisfied with the positioning, insert the stems.

· Garnish the bottom with clusters of pine cones, and, if you wish, wire on a green or red plaid bow.

14

Windows

IN WASHINGTON YOU KNOW fall has settled in when the wind creates enormous tree tosses and great sighs while the temperature drops precipitously, and every gust is followed by a rattling of dried leaves in the gutter. On the mall, the big old trees shake down torrents of leaves, and flocks of birds explode upward and wheel toward the south. Soon, sky is showing through the flowering plum outside the bay windows of my office, and you can see far.

I love the beneficial effects of cold and rain on the flowers after a hot summer. From my perch at the top of the steps to the kitchen, I monitor a flush of new growth, not unlike spring. Wax begonias grow big and bright, and the leaves of the geraniums in the porch baskets darken their greens. Petunias open new trumpets. This is

SEEING FAR

*In the language of flowers,
holly means
"foresight."*

their third blooming. My beloved 'Dark Opal' basil throws ever taller rose-pink flower spires, vying with mints to perfume the after-rain air. We harvest mums, asters, and blue salvias. In the kitchen and dining room sumptuous bouquets spread their fragrance — basil and mint, pink and purple asters, goldenrod, scarlet sumac, and plumy grasses from trips to the Shenandoah Valley. The rose-bushes throw new buds.

Views from my windows change almost daily, as they do in spring. But now vistas are opening up, leading the eye. The crusty, deeply crevassed bark of a venerable street tree invites contemplation, which expands to include the foliating bark of the neighbor's crape myrtle, then the white birch and sycamore beyond, then the crows' nests, one at the top of each tall shade tree between here and East Capitol. The unusual comes forward. The dawn redwood towering at the corner goes naked, as it does every year. The cardinal reappears, fluttering up from the viburnum to the flowering cherry, up and over to the dogwood berries, and finally to the top of the maple where it disappears against the blinding sun. The variegated holly with its spiny leaves and sparkling white margins readies berries that glow like Rudolf's nose.

As the year lumbers up to its longest night, December 21, the garden that grew tall and proud in spring and summer softens, shrinks, sinks toward the earth, reducing everything to essential, rich, nourishing, primal elements. I love the hush of the late garden. Summer cicadas give way to crickets. When the crickets fall quiet, you can hear the rustle of soft old leaves. Then real cold comes, and the trees creak. Standing in the garden, I think often of Sally. When she had passed age seventy-five, she announced one day that she preferred winter to all other seasons. "Because," she said, "you can see so much farther when all those leaves are gone."

Sally left this world one Saturday on her way to a bridge game in Boston after a four-star dinner party the night before. They told me she was driving along alone, and she would have felt a sudden headache bad enough to make her pull over to the side of the road. A state trooper found her. She never woke up. Earl and I were in New York making Sunday brunch when Sally's daughter-in-law phoned to tell us Sally was in the hospital in a coma. There was nothing I could do, she said, no point in coming. She promised to phone if there was any chance I could see Sally.

About ten days later, shutting the dinner roast into the oven, I found myself thinking of Sally, though not more that day than any other. She is usually close to my thoughts. Suddenly, I was swept by a feeling of great joy associated with her. I straightened up from the oven, surprised, and I know I was smiling. It seemed that Sally was skimming over meadows of daffodils. I felt Sally's laughter, the feeling of a very young woman laughing with joy. The feeling faded away, but left me happy about Sally. I supposed she had recovered. At about ten I was in bed reading, and Sally's daughter-in-law called me to say Sally had gone at about six o'clock that evening.

In the fall, they planted masses and masses of daffodils in a place Sally loved, a place with a far view.

CHRISTMAS IN THE FLOWER SHOP

THE closest I've ever been to Santa's workshop was Christmas season in the flower shop with Ruth and Peter. Peter Darmi and Ruth Manning were born to uptown Manhattan florists supplying the top-hat-and-tails trade in the 1920s and 1930s. Peter's dad sent him to study medicine at Cornell University, but Peter opted for flowers. Ruth's parents raised her in the luxury hotel that housed their flower shop, and it never crossed Ruth's mind to do anything but flowers. Ruth and Peter married and bought Hunter Flowers when the children and I lived next door in the rustic penthouse on the roof of 1049 Park Avenue.

At Christmas, the shelves, counters, and floor of the flower shop were jammed with poinsettias, evergreen wreaths, swags, and garlands. The aroma mingled spicy pine, spruce, eucalyptus, juniper, dark red roses in the refrigerated cases, Ruth's long black cigarillos, and barley broth bubbling on an electric ring in the back of the shop. Peter loves to cook, and florists don't have dinner until the last arrangement has been delivered. The closer we got to the holidays, the more frantic the phone orders and delivery boys became. Sometimes Ruth invited me to come downstairs to help replenish their supply of little boxwood topiary trees. It was one of their best-selling items.

We gathered in the back behind walls of poinsettias and cellophaned arrangements that were ready for delivery. Three tall stools were set around the big, nearly square work table. At each seat, Peter had placed several Oasis cones to use as bases for the topiary trees. The twelve-inch cones had been soaked in water containing floral preservative and were anchored in slightly tight ceramic holders or redwood boxes.

While Ruth and I settled down on our stools, Peter heaped branches of English boxwood in the middle of the table. One whole pound of it goes into a twelve-inch tree. Peter started by breaking off five-inch clusters of box and inserting them horizontally around the base of the cone. That set the width of the tree base at about ten inches, the proportion Peter prefers for a twelve-inch topiary. Next, Peter put the very top cluster in upright, a sprig three or four inches long. Then we filled in from the bottom up with progressively shorter clusters.

As each topiary was completed, Peter trimmed it with scissors to a near-perfect cone shape. Then we misted it with a florist's product that helps boxwood retain color and moisture. Home decorators often use hair spray. When all the trees were made — a dozen or so — we took a break. Ruth served rich, hot broth and ship's crackers. We'd munch and mumble a carol, struggle against laughter to remember all the verses of "The Twelve Days of Christmas," and answer the calls still coming in with orders from the West Coast.

The most wonderful part came last — decorating the little trees. Peter swept the cannibalized boxwood branches to the floor and cleared the table of everything but the topiaries. Ruth ransacked the shop, searching cubbyholes high and low for the minuscule toys and tree ornaments she and Peter had collected all year. I remember minute della Robia–style apples and pears, tiny bugles you could blow, drums, miniature gum drops, very small plaid bows. While Peter dusted some of the trees with silver or gold glitter, or imitation snow, we wired the ornaments and got them ready to press into the trees.

By then it was midnight. Peter kissed Ruth under a kissing ball. The phone was still ringing sporadically, the smoke from Ruth's cigarillo curled upward, the radio played carols — and we were surrounded by flowers, and making joyful little trees, and all was right with the world.

 # FLOWERS EVERY DAY

HOLIDAY DECORATIONS

Pretty Things

• Clusters of magnolia leaves and pine cones.

• Baskets filled with dried flowers and foliage, all frosted with florist's white spray paint.

• Long-stemmed wine-red roses tied with broad white satin ribbon.

• Green eucalyptus with long stems of miniature red carnations.

Centerpieces

• Three baby peach or white poinsettias in white coffee mugs, with drifts of tangerines on tufts of white pine.

• On a bed of hemlock and magnolia leaves, a scattering of red carnations surrounding tall dark red candles in silver candlesticks tied with red satin bows.

Ruth's Favorite Holiday Arrangements

• A silver Revere bowl packed with florist's Oasis anchored by fine chicken wire, and completely covered with sprigs of Oregon holly and white roses or red carnations. Ruth distributes the flowers unevenly in clusters — three or four here, five there.

• A low bowl packed with Oasis anchored by fine chicken wire, and covered with sprigs of balsam greens, white pine, and variegated holly. Ruth adds clusters of Lady apples and red carnations, or Christmas ornaments wired together.

Peter's Favorite Buffet Centerpieces

• In the center of the buffet, a low, round bowl filled with white roses, and a few sprigs of variegated holly with red berries. At either end of the table, Peter sets a boxwood tree decorated with morsels of glazed lemon and orange peel, and candied ginger — a North Carolina tradition.

• In the center of the buffet, a carousel whose base is a round wooden bowl filled with Oasis. The Oasis is an inch or so higher than the bowl, and Peter covers it completely with small, long-lasting red or white flowers, such as carnations or daisy mums. The floor of the carousel is set with seven or eight little figures — a horse, a tiger, a swan, an elephant, a soldier, buglers. The carousel posts are short wooden skewers spray-painted white.

Holiday Garlands

Peter made garlands of evergreens following the basic procedures described in the Flowers Every Day section of Chapter 6, and then varied them in the following ways:

GARLAND OF LIGHTS

· Make a garland of sprigs of aromatic evergreens garnished with bright-berried stems of holly.

· As you wire the garland, weave through it one or more strands of miniature white lights.

SANTA GARLAND

· Make a garland of sprigs of aromatic evergreens garnished with holly, and wire in dozens of small red carnations. The flowers will keep their color as they dry.

CHRISTMAS ROSE GARLAND

· Make a garland of sprigs of English boxwood, and work into it red rosebuds, individually wired. The garland will dry and hold its color for months.

Holiday Swag

At Chimney Hill we made cutting our own tree one of the family holiday traditions — and we still do. Like everyone else, we invariably miscalculate the height and drive home from the tree farm with more tree bouncing fore and aft of the car roof than the ceiling can take. The excess goes into the front door swag, wreaths, and the garlands that our daughter, Holly, winds up the banisters and drapes along the mantel of the fireplace. The black Chinese chest, year-round home to our bows and baubles, yields a huge red velvet bow to center the door swag. Sometimes it needs ironing. Once in a great while we make a new one.

· Foliage: Take two large, full branches of tree greens, and overlap the cut ends by six or eight inches. Bind them together firmly with a spool of heavy-gauge florist's wire. Don't cut the wire.

· Lay over these branches shorter stems of holly with the berries prominently displayed. Bind them together.

· Turn the swag over and make a loop of wire with which to hang the swag.

· Set a large red velvet bow over the wired stems at the center of the swag, and fix it onto the greens with fine wire.

· Wire tree baubles, Lady apples, small red pears, pine cones, or whatever you fancy, and attach on either side of the bow.

Peter's Kissing Ball

· With fine chicken wire, form a hollow ball, and stuff it with sphagnum moss soaked in water and squeezed out. Loop a wire through the center of the top for hanging the ball.

· Fill the ball with sprigs of greens from the tree, artemisia, and needled herbs such as rosemary, lavender, santolina.

· Wire a lush stem of mistletoe, and hook it into chicken wire in the middle of the underside of the ball.

· Hang the ball. Attach a soft red satin bow with long streamers to the top of the wire supporting the ball.

HAPPY NEW YEAR BOUQUET

Spray-paint white two tall twiggy branches, and stand them in a wide container to dry. With red embroidery silk or narrow red ribbon, tie on one white and two red helium balloons about a third from the top but at different levels. Add three Rubrum lilies, two red roses, red and white carnations, eucalyptus, and cedar or ferns, and fill out the bouquet with small white mums and purple statice. Tie on a big red satin bow.